To Li___

~joy!
Angie
xx

First published January 1993
by Zwitter Publishing
53 Beaconsfield Rd, St Margarets,
Twickenham, Middx. TW1 3HX.

Copyright c Gyerek 1993

Typeset in 10 point Times by
Zwitter Publishing

All rights reserved. No part of this book may
be reprinted or reproduced or utilised in any
form or by any electronic, mechanical, or other means,
now known or hereafter invented,
including photocopying and recording,
or in any information storage retrieval
system, without the permission in
writing by the publishers

ISBN 0 9520713 0 4

A CIP record for this book is available
from the British Library.

Printed in London by
Ad Graphics Group

CONTENTS

Universal Law	13
Art of Awareness	37
Mastering Self-Knowledge	51
Developing Judgement	65
Recognising Substance	77
Maintaining Understanding	91
Applying the Truth	103
Identifying Success	119
Easy Life	131
Index	153

To my Father

INTRODUCTION

If you are completely happy and able to handle all the ups and downs of life now, and in the future, then this book is not for you. Unfortunately there are very few of us who can claim such confidence, so a way to live without difficulty, disappointment and despair is described in this book. It may all sound a bit too easy, but the whole point is that it *should* be easy. It is wrong however to think that there will be no effort involved. To return to your *true* personality requires you to recognise the role of image in your life. This awareness enables you to completely enjoy all the things you have. You won't read this book and instantly change. But repeatedly reading and understanding yourself and your circumstances will certainly help.

Everything works in cycles, and, in this age of little awareness, our lives have become so dominated by image that money, success and the perfect relationship are expected. Image is now so powerful that it threatens our very ability to be ourselves. Most people have an idea of their image; in most of us this appears in the way we dress in our daily lives. There are many other types of confusing images however; religion, politics, science, mediums, crystals etc. These are less obvious types of image, but are in many ways far more powerful than dressing-up.

This is because peoples lives are led by, or even based on, such images (but to some even the attraction of dressing-up is overpowering). So why do people place importance on images? Because it removes the responsibility of how they appear to others; for instance the camouflage of a certain fashion, or a 'crutch' like politics, science, religion to explain things which they can't believe. They can then place these impressions on a different level, that of whichever of these convenient and useful images they have.

All these images have tried to create 'certain' explanations to take away the burden of the ups and downs of life, in return for some kind of affiliation, whether emotional or financial. All, however, have failed to create clarity and complete happiness and these very real images have only brought dissatisfaction because they all seem, at the beginning, so believable. Marriage, for instance; people feel safer after signing this contract, even when the divorce rate is so high.

This is one example, but there are many images surrounding us across the whole of our lives which have not worked. But consider what happens when there are no images at all and you look at the *real* feelings you have, rather than a convenient set of guidelines produced for you. This is not to remove these large images, because many could not survive without them, but for those of us who still have the ability to wonder, an easier life is possible. It starts with you questioning how these images *affect* you.

Even drunks or drug-takers are affected by image, so sober up long enough to find out if you can have an easy life without killing your personality. This is a personal choice and is not intended for groups of any kind. It may be different and difficult at first, as many of you may have been brought up within such images. But Gyerek found that life is a better place when you accept uncertainty.

Gyerek was a little boy without heroes, or a library, or any knowledge of the great thinkers of our time. All his life he searched for a way to have an easy life, only to find that after calling the natural product of his efforts *totalling*, some of the principles incorporated had been recorded two-and-a-half thousand years ago (to his knowledge) and were probably from far more ancient origins. What he had discovered was the lost art of combining; looking inwards at your own personality and using your senses to sample the world around you and to be happy in your place within it. These skills of insight and outsight are little practised for three reasons; first, very few people have these abilities and are willing to share them; second, most of us are too busy and it seems too difficult a task to embark on, until we have a personal problem which we wish to solve. Finally, it is not in the interest of people who wish to influence us to have large numbers of the population being able to take charge of their lives.

Many groups of people have, in the past, packaged these ideas for their own ends. Religious groups are by far the largest participants in this practice. Some of the central building blocks of Totalling have been twisted to suit the bias of different religious groups. Totalling is an individual process and unlike groups, it gives the power to the individual and is therefore the only way of substance. It removes all the religious and other images; the idols, the robes, the scientific methods, the promises and suggestions, for so long a convenient and consistent joke on humanity. Gyerek says joke because humanity is undermined by the way image mocks nature.

Gyerek was a follower of his thoughts and emotions, always travelling, rarely finding a suitable place to stop. So he stopped searching and started accepting, and slowly the universe touched his hand. He just felt that he knew who he was, and was happy with his place.

There was no longer the need to justify moving, as he realised that to move was to be alive and he wanted to live. If there were no movement, clouds would not bring rain, people could not go to work, so they could feed themselves, and there would be no making love and therefore no children.

Gyerek enjoyed writing down his thoughts in the knowledge that he could just leave his ideas for others to find, and, like any good nature-trail, the better totallers will understand much more than the less observant.

HOW TO READ THIS BOOK

To most, considering the whole of their life is an immense task. This is a shame, because they miss how simple and beautifully linked things are. But this is possible, if you peruse a number of topics which build into a practical way of discovering. For every reader, the amount of awareness this recreates will depend on their willingness to experiment within their thoughts and feelings. Gyerek recommends persevering and discussing your ideas with relatives and friends in a simple way, to gauge their point of view in relation to your new appreciation.

This book did not take a day to write and was returned to over and over again, so it may be useful to read a small amount at a time at a slow pace and try to understand what has been said before going on. Most important however, is that you do not overload yourselves with information. Just take it easy and enjoy the trail - it may be exciting and you may wish to see all of it, but it will still be there tomorrow, so do not rush and exhaust yourself. In this way you will be able to remember more and you can always read the book again. Gyerek wishes you to enjoy the journey, and hopes you achieve awareness.

Don't forget you can also refer to the relevant section of this book if you are emotionally excited, such as angry, in love, or impatient. It may not solve your immediate problem, but it will stop even bigger ones resulting from hasty actions. Relate these ideas to your own experience and enjoy the results.

Many simple examples are given, but these are not comprehensive as Gyerek would like to encourage your awareness by allowing you to identify and understand your own circumstances.

NATURE: ROOT OF REASON

This book is a big nature trail in which you can follow the thoughts and feelings of Gyerek, or move on and off the trail as you please. It is not designed to be a list of what steps you should take every day to make your life better; for that type of brain-washing there are many existing books. It is intended that each reader takes a voyage of discovery towards living life in the way in which they are happy, by *accepting* all the good and bad. The essential thing is that each person takes the journey and hopefully develops the type of life that suits them best. Central to any nature-trail is nature itself.

Nature is often mistaken for the sum of plants and animals around us, but this is a careless use of the word. It is really the intrinsic character of a thing, its essential quality and that which makes it different from all other things. It also refers to the physical power causing the phenomena of the universe. In the plant and animal world, biologists have spent many years classifying all the differences into species, but in the species 'man', the differences between individuals are so wide that Gyerek suggests 'man' should be classified by character, as well as biology, ie 'people' and 'humans'.

Gyerek feels that there are two sets of individuals. The first set are the 'civilised' individuals; these are called 'people' throughout this book. People's idea of being civil is to be polite, obliging and not rude, not military, not religious, not criminal, not political, and obey civil laws. The way that people organise themselves in day-to-day life, however, is the direct opposite of this description. People are impolite, unhelpful, rude, military, religious, political, and hypocritically take every opportunity to beat the system. People can be seen rushing, bumping into one another within urban centres.

The second set are 'uncivilised' individuals, who are called 'humans' throughout the book. Humans' idea of being 'uncivil' is to be impolite, unobliging and rude, aggressive, pagan, tribal, criminal, and to disobey the civil laws. Humans do not organise themselves in day-to-day life, but they are similar to people 'only' in the sense that they also behave in the opposite manner to their description. They are polite, helpful, unmilitary, unreligious, unpolitical, and honestly take every opportunity to live the way they feel, within the restrictions of civil law. Humans can equally be seen rushing in urban centres, but they don't bump into you. They are also comfortable with walking, swimming, working within the natural world. (People appear less comfortable within the natural world.)

Humans base their lives on an innate moral instinctive sense; an understanding of the condition of man, before society is organised. People have no such insight, and can therefore depend only on the images presented by 'civilised' life for their guidance.

Given that the majority of information received by people is packaged in powerful images, it is not surprising that people believe these images. If you are one of these people and are not prepared to look beyond them, this is a short book, and you will get from 'civilisation' what you deserve. If, however, you live in the 'civilised' world, but cannot understand why you are unsuccessful, or are unhappy with it, read on.

To remove a dependence on image you must identify your own character. This is difficult, because we are faced not only with the problem of working out ourselves, but also with a wealth of external information from other people and our surroundings. If you cannot recognise how you feel, you leave yourself at the mercy of your own whim, and the compassion of others. So at some point you have to choose; ignorance, or awareness. If you choose ignorance, how will you discover what you are happy with, suited to, and wish to protect for another day? There is a formula waiting in each of us, in which we can discover what we are happy with. It is a very simple formula, as it allows for everyone to be themselves.

Some people are happy working with people, others using technology to be more efficient, others using their hands to make things, others doing anything to make money and yet others only doing things they consider to be right. As long as this is honest for them and clear to others, all is well whatever they choose, but if there is the type of conflict - so often the case in our work, with friends or family or within ourselves - this imbalance creates stress, unhappiness and regrets for our actions and the time wasted. Life is far too short already to present ourselves with such an unfair burden. The only reasonable answer is to be yourself and accept your nature, and in doing so you have the best opportunity to use and develop further all the unique skills you have.

To look at nature, (to remind you again; this encompasses everything in the known universe, and each thing's unique qualities) we have been given faculties, thoughts, feelings and the senses of sight, hearing, taste, touch and smell. So many people put on a Walkman and blot out experience, while just a few use their senses to sample the world around us, to know where they are, wherever they are. If this tendency continues, people in the future will be unable to observe anything, because successive generations will be less capable of using their facilities.

Fundamental to humans is the ability to acquire information. This sampling can be organised to produce thoughts, rules and principles, such as in science, or for most - in a less organised fashion - giving feelings, ideas and imagination; this allows them to become closer to their attachment to the resources that support and nourish them (and that does not mean supermarkets!).

All of nature has roots. For most plants, it is the part connected to the ground, the part which provides nourishment. For people these roots are not physically connected to the ground, they are connected to beliefs and the information they discover with their faculties, you *are* your information. How did you come to believe that Columbus sailed across the Atlantic to discover America? Why does it rain? How were you brought up? Where are you now and what are the the daily influences reinforcing these things?

The thinking process of reasoning has created many ideas; Gyerek himself at times has even been tempted to express himself within the way intellectuals twist philosophy by saying 'it is, therefore I am'. This differs from the more popular saying 'I think therefore, I am', in that your surroundings give you the references for thought (if you need to prove that your surroundings exist, Gyerek recommends falling over; did it hurt?). We do think and we like to order those ideas. But reason is greater than just thought. It is a less tangible thing more difficult to explain, a thing of substance which makes us do things. On most occasions it is more than just thinking which drives us to do things, it is our feelings, and Gyerek does no more than help the individual enjoy this expression.

Gyerek does not require or encourage an audience, and there is no society or organised meetings for totallers; just the comfort of being yourself. This is a purely selfish activity, aiming to allow totallers the ability to recognise the reason in their surroundings and the characteristics which make them unique - and therefore the ability to develop themselves. One of the main techniques involved is to learn how to observe yourself doing and producing and then drawing conclusions from that process. You then no longer need gods, expensive counsellors, or concern for anything other than those concerns you choose. This journey is not designed to change your financial circumstances, though this may be the result, for better or worse. What will happen is that you will be able to concentrate on yourself as a fixed point of reference, to be able to look at your world and how you wish to work within it, and as a consequence you will understand the people and the world around you more.

The first step towards making life easier is to accept the processess that affect all natural phenomena. These processes and cycles influence and fuel nature, the universe, the earth (including soil and plants and animals etc) and you. If you are bored by how nature works in your surroundings, how can you expect to discover or be excited about your own nature? Your environment is the fundamental part of your daily life, as it provides food, air, space, resources; in fact everything you need for life.

UNIVERSAL LAW

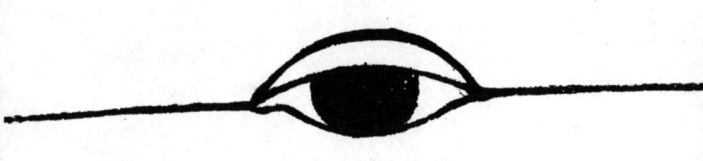

POLARITY

Polarity is the force of positive and negative which recreates movement.

The forces which lead all our lives and the things around us are the forces of positive and negative. These are most easily seen in the extremes around us; light and dark, hot and cold, large and small, rich and poor, safe and dangerous, sick and healthy, happy and sad and for better or worse. These are opposites and it is the tension between them which recreates all the differences and movements between positive and negative.

For example, one place where positive and negative work together to produce movement is easily seen on a weather map. There are areas of high and low pressure and the air moves from the high towards the low, which produces the wind. In a similar way there are highs and lows, pluses and minuses throughout your life. Beauty can only exist because there is ugliness, good because there is bad, and therefore all these differences are connected together, always moving, and cannot be separated.

Positive and negative are independent, but understanding that they are together and always moving makes you see them, and yourself, as unstoppable. Positive and negative are also not held to any scale as they appear in the smallest particle, the most subtle emotion and the greatest processes in the universe. Slowly getting to know polarity will enable you to link the positive and negative in your life, producing a recognition of the speed and direction of the movement between your successes and losses. Too many are quick to see the negative. If you see the importance of each, you are no longer separate or frightened by them.

The whole of nature, the universe, the earth and all life which includes you and your character are described throughout the rest of the book as *all things*. If you wish to begin to understand how polarity effects all things, you have to begin to sample extremes. The first and easiest extreme is to learn how to be still. This is very difficult, as most people think that this time would be better spent by attacking any problems they have straight away instead of wasting time. But try it; go to a quiet room on your own and just sit for as long as it takes to get interested in doing something. It does not matter if the lights are on or off, just sit. You will find your mind becomes full of the things you wish to think of, things you wish to forget and more things which make you wonder how they got there at all.

The next task is to write all these things down; keep doing this until your head is completely empty. Don't worry, it is very difficult to forget everything and even if you can for a while, all the thoughts you had will soon return.

Once you have an empty mind, you can present it with the original problems, one at a time, or go into your everyday world and use your senses to see things afresh. If practised, the black and white in situations can be seen; later, if followed, shades of grey can be slowly identified. The lives of others, the way you feed yourself, the way you affect the earth, the way the earth affects you, the way the earth is in the universe and the way the universe depends on nature for its very existence. If you do nothing for a while, polarity begins to work and you can identify the *opposite* of stillness. Be still and see movement, then move and remember what it was like to be still.

By doing this you will have stopped trying to push back the limit of your mind; you will be making space to think and feel. Your first two skills, therefore, are thinking in black and white and being able see how movement is important to you. Through the rest of the journey, it is possible to collect many such skills along the way, but not all are so clearly spelt out. So you will need an open mind and this is the start of the nature-trail. You will be on the road to observing and participating more fully in your life.

There is really only one way to an easy life and that is to let things happen, to discover your individuality and the way you relate to all things. To recreate an easy life you need to discover your uniqueness and this can only be achieved on your own. All the information you receive from others, whether requested or not, will only present you with images, eg religion, science or magic. Remember they are looking for followers to support their view. Freed from the need to follow, you are able to take the information you want and then think and feel for yourself, crossing any of the disciplines mentioned in whichever way you see fit.

Freed in such a way, you can choose your own echoes from magic, science, religion, and pure fun; science can produce useful structures for classifying phenomena; magic, religion and fun can nourish your feelings and it is you who chooses to bring the positive and negative in each alive. Nature provides the force for existence, and the universe the space for all things to have their place.

INFINITY

There is no beginning or end to nature

Up to now the limits of our knowledge have been bounded by a scientific insistence that we must base all our knowledge on material testing, looking for things that repeat. The way science discovers is by using the standard method of investigation. This system contains the following progression; aim, apparatus, method, result, conclusion and feedback system, which allows results to be acceptable, and therefore 'real', when the result for a particular test can be obtained over again. Science has based these methods on the number systems, which are accepted by mathematicians.

So it is not a surprise that science has been unable to provided the answers to the important questions - such as why we are here, how can we enjoy ourselves, and where can we get a vegetarian pizza with wine for under £2?

But seriously - for all the thousands of years of interest and searching, no solutions to the questions of why nature, the universe, the earth, or man exists have been found. Gyerek thinks that the reason for the lack of answers, is that the units used by mathematicians are arbitrary, man-made and not related to the subject being studied i.e. nature. The single unit which is the basis of all calculation is impersonal; it has no relationship with other units. Let me explain. In mathematics one unit plus one unit equals two.

That is fine within man-made systems such as money, £1 + £1 = £2. But this does not work in nature as there are relationships between individuals. For example, if you bring together one male and one female, there is a relationship and the ultimate conclusion is a child, in this case 1 + 1 = 3. When other individuals are brought together (eg fish) one's relationship with another could result in thousands of individuals. Mathematicians cannot get answers to the questions in nature unless they understand that in nature, single units are different. No man-made unit will therefore account.

The only units to be used are those found in nature itself, even though these may seem more difficult to use. Freed from the unnatural method of counting, you can just use your thoughts, feelings and senses to experience, and work, within nature's units. If the only thing you get from this book, for the short time you read it, is the ability to challenge your existing views, then it will have been a useful experience.

The universe is a big thing and we know little about it. Many scientists would dispute this, but the fact of the matter is that we have never seen a sun like our own outside our galaxy. So we don't know if there are other galaxies and we don't know where space ends. So if scientists know some things, they are relatively small, compared with what we would wish to know. Gyerek thinks that space and time end where and when we no longer have the ability to influence. When you appreciate this you do not use time thinking about things that are beyond anyone's acknowledgment. You just get on with your life like the rest of nature having the ability to be aware of what is real, and enjoying it. The universe is infinite, but it may only be infinite in time, as space expands and contracts to fit.

MATTER IS

Matter and energy cannot be created or destroyed

There are many parts to the elements that make up people and everything around them. Scientists have classified these; one of the first and most important of their observations is that all things cannot be created or destroyed. In the same way you are the combination of your thoughts and feelings and these cannot be created, or destroyed; they just keep *changing*, continuously being modified and stressed by people and the situations which occur. Use your senses to identify, in your own life, what is matter and what is image. Getting down to the solid basis; the things around you that only change in their compostion.

This allows you to take an active part in, and responsibility for, events. The value of this is great; you will start working on your own and with others to produce the best circumstances for life. People are always trying to explain the question of the universe. The most widely accepted conclusion on the formation of the universe is the Big Bang theory. But why do scientists have such debate on the Big Bang theory of the formation of the universe? This theory says that the universe was created in one great explosion, while the origin of this matter, or why it moved away from the original explosion, are left unexplained!

So where did the matter which formed the universe come from? Nowhere of course; we have already found that the best of our scientists believe that matter cannot be created or destroyed, so was Einstein wrong? The universe has always had elements and processess which have existed, large or small, forming and reforming. All the chemicals and their combinations are dependent on movement to develop. This movement is a result of the universe expanding and contracting. Because this is difficult to identify and the universe takes up such a large space, we are nervous or even scared by it. This is because we cannot have enough information in our heads at one time to understand it.

But it is not something to be scared of, and should never have been. Having a large amount of space allows all things to exist and have the room they need to move, and allows for development or destruction. How many times have you been in a crowd of people shopping, or in a subway, and felt you would be far more able to move and to get where you wanted if you had space to avoid them? All things travel, even emotions, so the way you travel will affect your speed and direction and the way all things move in relation to you; if you are erratic, erratic events will happen etc. Movement allows things to grow and also contract; knowing this and you won't always expect growth. Allowing for failure removes vast expectations and gives you the emotional space to live.

SPACE

Matter is located in space

We are all dependent on the earth and its relationship with the universe, and all things which affect the universe. But we generally consider only our own space and how other people affect it. Equally important, however, are the wider issues of why and how each of us is affected by the world around us and the people on it. These wider issues could threaten the small piece of space we believe we have sole use of.

Consider the space in your life, the distance, the places and also the time between events. You are always using space at work and at play; take account and see it for what it is. Knowing the value of space allows you to have a balance in the way you approach it, and will give you the ability to make the room to live rather than only having tasks. Relationships suffer this problem, but often the reaction to a lack of space is to escape, rather than to make room; for instance it is possible to live in one room with someone and never see them, because they are there when you are not.

There are also concerns about the way we use the environment, but these issues are not just global, and while they are only thought of in this way, unseen, the real limits of space are slowly forcing us into man-made corridors; the motorways, the pavements and the estates. Most of the problems we suffer are caused by no longer being close to, and able to survive from, the land. When you know this, you have a chance to reduce any lifestyle problems by remembering the importance of free space and movement.

The room within which each of us lives is of great interest and we often change the way we use it to meet our needs for relaxation, entertainment, self-development, sleep, eating, fun and a wealth of other things. The space between us, which is available for us to use, is priceless, as it often makes us who we are. Consider a house; it is the holes in the walls which make the doors and windows, which make the room more than a cupboard. It is often the things which are missing which make a thing complete. What things do you need, what could you usefully lose? Think about the last time you moved house and the commodities which you really need will become more obvious. The possessions you need are important, but only if they are appropriate; some people need more than others to live, but often less than they imagine.

The method to guarantee space is the same, both physically and mentally. Space is only available if there is no clutter. Lack of clutter in possessions, and thoughts, is essential if you wish to move in your thoughts, feelings and deeds, and movement is living. Space allows the movements that you are able to make to be expressed; be careful with space and you will not restrict yourself.

REFORMING

In nature nothing is still; it grows, it dies and is born again

The universe, the earth and you are always moving, so why feel worried when things change? Nature takes opportunities which are in tune with the situation, so why shouldn't you? Lions do not grow in soil, cars do not drive on water, so why should you live in situations which are not right? But trees must fall before grass will grow, so you may have to destroy the old difficult situations to create a way closer to your character. But everything else in the universe reforms, so why don't you? Being able to throw away the unwanted or unsuccessful is a skill which will also stop those dramatic problems.

When you work at the same job for twenty years, and that job disappears, there are many problems. But if you did not base the whole of your well-being on only one thing in the first place, you would not receive that displeasure. Depending on one thing - income, relationships, etc - only produces a future insecurity. You do not have only one source of enjoyment or pleasure; Gyerek thinks that even though it may be easy for a while, you may never completely depend on one thing for your emotional security, or your livelihood.

Chemicals do not combine unless they naturally have the ability to do so; they form existing materials and sometimes when the circumstances are right, they can on their own, or with the help of people, form new ones. As long as chemicals only combine as is right for chemicals, there is no problem. If chemicals did things unnaturally, as people do, the physical world where we live would be as stressed as people.

Existence comes from non-existence. This would seem to support the big bang idea, but as in any big bang a child does not exist until he or she is conceived and born. So your own character, if you don't know it already, has been born and is waiting to be discovered. All you have to do is make the time, have the inclination and direction to find it. For people, this is where the problem starts. They are always so busy; rushing here and there. No time or appreciation; but they would argue, why should they?

CYCLES

Everything moves in cycles

Your character is going on, whether you recognise it or not. You have bad points and good ones and that's ok as long as you are not concerned by this. In just the same way the earth has what seems like very destructive processes, such as earthquakes, and very good things like producing crops. Nature is not good or evil; chemicals are what they are and they just get on with it. They have no problems, because they do what they are best at, or able to do.

They behave like little children, before the temptations of the people world; the advertising, and peer groups, weak and without expectation and without any other purpose than doing. In that way they age, die, and recreate once more. The only way this greatness can be observed is the seemingly effortless and unstressed way things act. When you are yourself, this effortlessness will equally be seen in your actions. Accepting the effortless way of working enables you to know when you are putting too much effort in and not getting much in return. If you are aware of the value of the things you do and the effort used to do them, you will be very efficient and effective; do what comes easily, because it's what you do best.

Things then seem magnificent - and they are - as there is no pretence. This is a great feeling which is more than ordinary. Then again, this feeling comes and goes; you can be in touch with yourself for *some* of the time. But it is the times you are *not* in touch with yourself which help you to know and appreciate when you *are*. A feeling, a person, the earth, the universe, and nature itself all contain cycles which grow too old and return to seed to grow again.

MOVEMENT

Nature expands and contracts, which provides movement

The most important route to understanding your own nature and that of all things is through honesty. Nature is honest, the universe and the earth do what is theirs to do. It is easy to begin to understand the nature of things when you return to basics; the stars and planets move from the centre to grow and then return to nothing. This movement away from the centre of our universe causes the movement of the earth and the earth's movement affects the climate and even the ways we feel. On a hot muggy day everything is too much effort! Knowing this constant movement gives an indicator of how far from your centre you are. This produces comfort, as you know on any particular day that you are up or down, close or far from what you like doing. This finally allows you to take on new and creative ideas and situations when you are ready and therefore reduces the likelihood of failure.

The way things come together may change, but the physical processes remain the same. In the universe this means matter - the stars, the planets - and what is on the planets expands to fit the available space. It is like a photocopier; if you enlarge during a photocopy the space

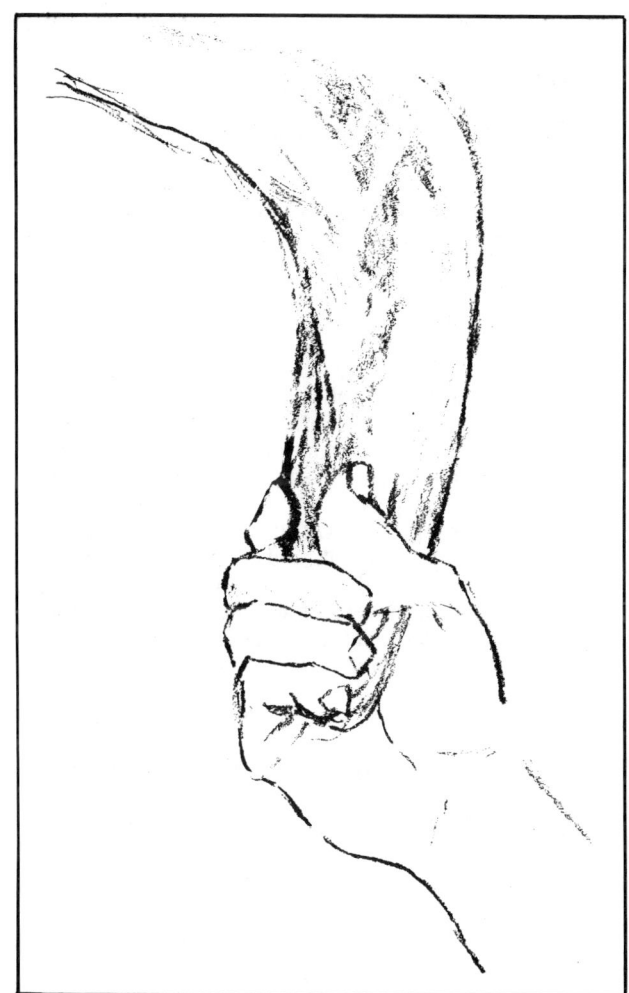

between the dots increases, so that eventually you get a very grainy look and you can see the position of the individual dots.

When you reduce the same photocopy the dots keep on condensing and the resolution becomes more and more intense until you get a single dot. It is not one dot of course, but we cannot see well enough to view it any other way. In people, character and experiences will expand in the same way as things affect them, generating feelings and thoughts along the way which may seem either positive or negative.

On earth it is only people who have thought and feelings who get confused about their role, and then spread this confusion into things they influence, as humans are keen to integrate with their surroundings. This is where unnatural actions of people start from, and the way you can see how far people are from their true nature. However, as people are part of nature, these unnatural actions are really as natural, so they are part of existence and should be accepted as such. If you use your senses you will see your movement and the way others move. This will give you the choice to sometimes go along with others or move in your own way.

If you don't move you are dead, deprived of experience and also the ability to recreate new life. Vast debate on existence is therefore meaningless and a waste of effort. Think only of the way you are and come closer to behaving like nature - your nature.

Moving is more than an exploration of time and the reason for space; it is a most useful object for identifying the important things in your life. We all have time, it is more valuable than money, because time is what we use to get money. We all choose to *spend* our time on many things; some people spend time only to buy daily tasks which are enough to feed themselves, other do activities which provide enjoyment and risk going hungry. In each case our lives always turn out related to how we spend time on a daily basis. If you wish to spend your time being a doctor you would train as a doctor today; so you could spend your time in the future being a doctor and earn money to support yourself. The way you move however is never that easy.

There are also risks attached to the way we move. We move to work by foot at 4mph with urban life around us; by train we travel at 60mph, by car up to 70mph, with other cars all around us. We move in planes at up to 1,200mph at an altitude where we cannot breathe,;for the majority just to see a better climate for 2 weeks. The human body can be injured at walking pace; it can also be hurt by the way we emotionally commit ourselves. Remember the doctor above; what if he could not afford to spend his time training. This hurt could be remembered far longer than a physical injury. We move, we take risks; choose the risk you take, don't forget a risk is there!

CHAOS

Things are only stable for a while

Keeping in touch with nature means accepting being comfortable with *not* being comfortable. We spend our lives always trying to be comfortable. That nice house, that nice car etc; in fact people do everything to get as far away from nature as possibly because they consider nature is unpredictable; humans accept nature as it is. This acceptance of people-made solutions is widespread.

When we look at our watches we believe that we know the time. But who created this time? People did, of course, for their own convenience. But ask yourself, from where does this time originate? It is really a method of measuring movements, which are themselves governed by nature. The best clocks are merely computers which calculate the movements of the planets or the movements of atoms. So even in our most strongly-held view of what is normal, it is merely a useful measurement of nature.

No matter how hard people try to stabilise life, it is all dependent on natural underlying processes, so you would do well to remember and consider this when you think about making stable; possessions, business, beliefs, events, or relationships. It is easier to have nothing than something, and remembering this removes the disappointment of plans not working. Accepting this truth will help you make more reasonable plans which will have a greater likelihood of success; you will be known as a realist rather than a dreamer.

Problems arise for people when they cannot understand that nature can have things which are always present, but behave chaotically, at random. When things behave in such a subtle and irregular way people become scared and revert to things which they think are constant. All of which are merely images, supernatural creations to take away the concern raised by the events of nature. Chaos is a part of nature and existence, and no end of faith in something or someone is going to alter how it is.

It was learned a long time ago that you cannot stop the tides, so why not just accept events as they happen, for good or bad, and face them honestly? Nature does not do anything it doesn't want to; it does not complain and no animal or plant complains to it. Only in the case of people is there complaint about their lot. All the things around you are comfortable, because they do not have to think about their circumstances or any reason for doing anything. The planet we live on is a big place and though it is getting smaller with better transport, there is enough space to move. The world is big enough for all; we don't have to be somebody we are not, for some image created by someone we don't even know. Unless of course that is our nature.

NON-AGITATION

Governing the speed of events reduces the intensity at which they happen

However ordered and successful your life may seem, all accomplishments will have some imperfection, or will last for a shorter time than expected. But if you are skillful, successful and honest, as in some way we all are, this ability will not go away and will always be available to be successful again when the time and conditions are right. If the economy changes, relationships move on; enjoy them and don't get over-excited by these movements, even when they are difficult to fathom.

Understanding this gives you an ability to excite yourself when you are lazy, and the confidence to slow down situations when they are unreasonably fast.

Events are as solid as physical things like towns. The space between events is like the distance we travel between towns. Most of us just want to get from one place to another, but the journey may often be more enjoyable than the arriving. However, we do not see the beauty along the way, because of our impatience to get to where we want to be. Everything comes from knowing nothing, being open to experience all your life and enjoying all parts of it. What if the earth sub-consciously decided to like winter and ignore all the other seasons; think of the loss. If you can enjoy all your movements and try to be as close to your good and bad points as possible, your potential cannot run out or finish, as it will always be with you.

This has been translated in religion to say God is everlasting. But in the dictionary, God is a supernatural being. In the bible it says that God created man in his own image, or was it the other way around? Anyway, if that is the case, look in the mirror and what do you see? God of course. You see the outer appearance of your face and body. What you look like is only a surface image which has no substance, and those who concentrate on this image are their own gods; however much religious leaders twist their words.

Animal intelligence is tested in many ways. Testing problem-solving in mice etc, while more intelligent animals such as monkeys can make simple tools. The only test which puts human beings (and dolphins) at the top of the intelligence ladder is that they can understand a joke. However, people are not so intelligent that they can understand the joke played on them by believing images. Most people can understand toilet humour. But try and tell a joke about people's beliefs, and it is not quite as funny. To understand that kind of joke requires a knowledge found behind the image; some substance inside a person that allows them to think and feel about things beyond images, beyond being consumers of easy ideas and material possessions. As this is a bit too much effort for most people, there seems to be creation of some kind of inverted knowledge.

Any idea which is different to people, and challenges the illusions of their world, is somehow wrong and this slowly produces a rigidity within them. This rigidity which is so set, in such a narrow fashion, will be broken sometime, like a tree falling in a high wind. Therefore different thoughts and feelings often seem stupid, but if you can say *I am stupid*, you may be able to learn again.

The events and thoughts we all have are very confusing and the more that happens to us, the more difficult things seem. So we have to return to simple things to make sense of our actions. These are as sure as, say, if you jump up and down when you're cold, you will became hot. If you exercise your feelings and thoughts in the same way, the problems you suffer from, like the cold, will be more comfortable.

Movement in your brain and your body generates the heat for life, and being able to be still sometimes reduces the speed of this activity, so you have time to be quiet when you want, or make something, paint, dig the garden, without any time constraint or concern for events, even just for 10 minutes. This is again a good starting point and a way to discover balance of action, through non-excitement. Let me give an example; take a bath - why is the water hot? The reason is that water is made up of one atom of hydrogen and two atoms of oxygen, hence H_2O. Each atom has an electron orbiting a central nucleus. Water becomes hot due to these electrons receiving energy from gas or electricity and then travelling faster, as they are excited. The same is true of situations, if more people or events add to a situation; it speeds up to the point that you could equally burn yourself. The same idea applies in both cases to slow things down; do nothing and it will cool.

But the difficulty is that to feed yourself you need to get excited, just like you warm-up before exercise. This is a most delicate balance, however, as you do not have to concentrate on how much water your body retains because your brain controls the process of biological balance (homoeostasis); this also operates within your thoughts and feelings and through totalling this is sometimes recognisable and sometimes not. Remember to be open-minded and caring in the situation, and you will always do what's right for you.

EVENTS AND YOU

Day to day things happen

We all face great pressures everyday; Gyerek is not an idealist and has all the usual hassles, the rent, food, bills etc but lives successfully in this way. Of course there are problems; at work investors require returns, at home relationships require give-and-take and leisure provides enjoyment. Sometimes, work in particular puts on such intense pressure that Gyerek wonders how he would cope without such awareness.

He remembers however, that these are only pressures, which at this time he has chosen. We can influence the intensity of the events which affect us, and act in a way which is ok for us. Balance your load and take your time when you need to. In this way you can find, and keep, your personality and events together, while finding a balance and approaching situations at a speed which is acceptable to you.

It is so easy to be affected by distraction, usually money, family problems, that wonderful holiday, that next night out, or having just too much to think about. But it is possible to participate fully and remain true to your thoughts and feelings, to be flexible and alive in your mind. You will know this by asking yourself if you can still display childish emotion, to do the things you would enjoy - those silly things - without thought of how it would look to others. Can you rethink all your inner concerns and opportunities and ties? Can you say, in confusing situations, what would I have done if I did not take all this time thinking about it? See things as they really are and not how you think they should be.

Don't close your mind to any idea or suggestion; be submissive, again remind yourself to be comfortable with chaos. Destroy all the distractions and hard-headed views which get you into trouble. Start to wonder again, and look at the way you really fit in. Decide how you do business; we have all found that living on credit removes our ability to do anything. You only end up working for someone else.

This is not just a financial habit, it is also an emotional one. When you constantly give or receive, the imbalance will mean that you live for someone else. You could be innovative and go forward without prejudice and without the need for any other support other than your own. Look at the events in which you play a part and ask yourself, who benefits? This is one of many of the questions you can ask yourself, when you are interested in awareness.

THE ART OF
AWARENESS

MASTERS

These are the truly honest ones.

Gyerek has respect for honest individuals. These individuals have knowledge so great that their reason and conclusions depend on nothing. Very few could hope to understand such a strangely confident uniting of thought and feeling. People do not understand them and can only see their image. They are aware, alert, courteous, informative, unfashioned, undistracted, interesting, patient and efficient. This combination of characteristics cannot be found in people; Gyerek has only ever seen some of these special qualities in humans, but never in such completeness. How far are *you* from this? The knowledge that perfection is being yourself, and everything else is caused by inefficiency, leads you by self-development to the stage where people cannot ignore your true worth.

There is a split in what we consider to be the behaviour of nature; all things, the universe, the earth, plants and animals, human beings and the behaviour of people. People typically consume, and try to play with nature, constantly trying to overcome and change the environment. Humans accept that their knowledge is not great enough to know the consequences of altering nature. They hope to live within their own nature, to be themselves, and to utilise the earth's resources, not consume them. But people have always developed civilisations with gods, which conveniently places an image in the place of the beautiful and diverse systems which result from nature. This image removes people's responsibility for the events that befall them.

It says in the Bible that the meek shall inherit the earth. The Chinese think that the weak are the strong ones, as they could experience everything. The American Indians believed that the earth was alive - even the rocks - and they were right, because at some time all rock on the earth's surface has evolved from somewhere else; either lava, or other rocks, or from organic processes; therefore they all move and are alive.

These ideas have historically been seen as unreasonable, blasphemous, or even as downright witchcraft, but only one who is scared or who wishes to control would describe others' ideas in such a way, preventing these thoughts and feelings from being experienced, placing limits on the way we behave, think, and feel.

So who are the masters? We all have a sense that there is 'something else', but what is it? A typical father-like image of God is as likely as a spaceman, or a bog-eyed monster. All of which are equally *unlikely*. What Gyerek knows is that if you decide on nothing, there may be no answers today, (but this is acceptable anyway) but you will certainly be more open to answers than if you believe a people-made preconception.

Who are the masters? Gyerek feels that the masters are truly honest humans who have no assumptions. Humans are so unusual that people cannot understand them and have to try and give them an image.

Gyerek believes Christ was probably one of these honest men, but people had to explain his honesty through a religious practice.

Gyerek cannot be sure of this, however he would like to meet or be, an honest human without any misguided images being attached.

FINDING YOUR WAY

Having the choice of being lost, with or without a map

So how do you begin to find out who you are? It is essential to be able to forget, to be able to be lost. This is obviously not easy, as the reason you picked up this book may have been because you have something you cannot forget. You will, however, if you spend time accepting things as they are, slowly remove things from your mind and become more comfortable. You can then have the choice of knowing your personality, or forgetting it, to find it again. Begin to use your senses; you must look around with as few burdens, financial, emotional or other, as you can and just be for a while.

Using your senses helps you notice many of the less obvious things, making you more perceptive and giving you the competitive edge. Many people would argue that improving your memory can produce greater happiness and self-awareness. Gyerek thinks that working hard in this way produces little gain. The more facts in your head, the more you think you know. If this process continues you come to believe you have command of the facts. This factual clutter reaches the point that people become inflexible, stuck in their own beliefs and assumptions. Gyerek thinks that, by reducing the amount you have in your head, you leave more space to think, feel and observe, and this is the way to stay alive.

If you understand this flexibility, don't work at it. Tick over like a slow-running engine. Move, be running, without effort. Do not present yourself with tasks, other than those which are absolutely necessary. Give yourself have the time to observe how your life works. Watch your ups and downs, the way things operate around you, in your life and in your surroundings. Look at how the world works with good sources of information. This means books and journals. Newspapers and television do not give simple reliable information. These media have increasingly become dominated by sensation, and propaganda. You should be aware of what is currently happening on a daily basis. But the daily media available is extremely general, and often misleading. It certainly would not help you with getting to know your nature, or that of your surroundings.

The key to really understanding how things around you are different from each other is to work out how you feel about the cycles of the earth, not just day and night, the weather and seasons, but also how you grow plants and how other animals live. Return to being still and knowing that everything is not that big; that everything returns to nothing.

Plants and animals die and are put in the soil and Gyerek believes even the universe itself will die and another will be born. Nature is unchanging. It is like a running track, you move, but the start and finish are in the same place. Be friends with this idea of constancy, and with an open heart you need not behave in any other way than that which is true to you. Then use your senses - your eyes, ears, and thoughts, to be aware what sort of individual you are. Being at one with yourself and all things is honest; that is why it is an easy life. Maybe you want to be a millionaire and will do anything to achieve this, while your true nature is to be a nurse, or the other way around.

You don't have to try all your life; if you listen to yourself you may be able to do what you feel all the time and be happy; so don't assess yourself on material measures of success. Your way of happiness is sustainable; by following your feelings, your nature, you will be alive during your life.

UNITING WITH NATURE

Being yourself and living in the real world

To start to live you have to learn to be gentle on yourself. You are competent at the things you know, perhaps despite any lack of encouragement or financial success. So why be violent, angry, or vengeful? Just be confident; you do not have to overstate your position, but be comfortable within it. Get to grips with using what you know, doing what you are good at and enjoying your ability. Your life is only the things that you do; if you only have work and always talk about that, that will *be* your life. Recognise that if you slightly change the basis of your living, you can subtly, or radically change your life. The consequence is that a better use of time will change the way you live. Having this ability will help you change your life should you wish, or need to.

People do not understand humans, so do not put effort into explaining yourself, unless you wish to deal with their prejudice. Any explanation will need an interpretation of nature. To describe the difference between how people and humans live; if you wish to save that time, direct them to this book. Living and working with people requires you to understand them and still know nature. The world people have created have lots of opportunities. Use them.

By being human and recognising your unique character you could develop an entirely new and productive role within it, but then again you may live in their civilisation long enough for you to gain resources to physically feed yourself. That is *your* choice. If however you have it all by uniting with your nature and still having a role with people, then this is the ultimate unity.

THE WAY OF NATURE

Discovering your personality and the world around you is an independent activity

This concentration on yourself must be seen in balance with the feelings you have for others. To care for others is not a sacrifice as long as you are in touch with your feelings, and caring does not become a burden. Allow things to happen by giving them a chance, but never be anything but honest and uncompromising. If you are in any situation which you find stressful, be aware of it. Also be aware that friends, relatives and acquaintances do not

always have the good sense to communicate with you on how they are coping. So always pay attention to gain understanding, and then act with certainty. Even if your actions seem hard, by having listened in the first place and having honesty in your heart, you will always be faced with a smile. (Even if you're wrong!)

This trust in yourself is difficult. However, by not following your thoughts and feelings, you will be planting seeds of problems which will grow and grow in the future. It may seem harder today, but it is better to face the smaller problem now than a big one tomorrow.

It is necessary to feel new and adventurous and to understand your good points, but most of all to realise that your bad points are useful to keep; for your bad points further help you understand the good. Illuminate your character by being yourself and always believing in yourself, and slowly you will move towards understanding nature, both your own and that of all things.

By experiencing more, you become aware of the simplicity and complexity of you and your surroundings. By the time you begin to understand this greatness, don't be surprised or concerned by the keen sense of humility and humbleness you feel. Keep moving and doing, and by allowing this honest movement, the types of resources you really want begin to be recognised.

These may at this starting point be out of reach for financial reasons, but at least you will now know what you like and what's available. Be sure of your nature and allow it to command you; for such little effort as getting to know yourself will produce maximum gains, better work and you will be far happier.

INSIGHT

Making hidden truth visible.

By noticing your daily actions, you will also be capable of helping others recognise theirs, but helping others needs thought. The best policy is to be cautious, firstly, because some people just look helpless to get assistance; secondly, some will take anything offered, because it seems free; thirdly, helping others can too easily become a habit and you will have no time for yourself.

Help must be based on need or something, so if you have to put effort into having things, be aware of how much you waste with tasks and people, in the the name of progress.

Finally, you take a risk by helping; what if the help you offer is not what is needed, or even makes the situation worse and puts you in danger? The only way to remove these problems is to develop the ability to remove assumptions. The sort of assumptions meant by Gyerek are: assuming you know the solution straight away, that you know what others are thinking and that you know what others are capable of doing. You can remove the tendency to assume if you remember that situations can end in another way. If you are able to remove these assumptions and then trust yourself, nothing is impossible and you will remove the limits imposed on you. When you have removed these boundaries, you will be far more open-minded and able to communicate with people and other humans. You will be fit to do greater things. Insight will always keep a channel open to see beyond image, to see both your own and others' substance. Start to recognise the difference between people and humans.

It is never enough just to go along; it is acceptable to sometimes drift like a boat on a river, without rowing, or rudder; to let the river take you where it will. But it is stupid not to watch where you're going. Rivers have waterfalls, rapids, fallen trees etc, which can be avoided if spotted. It is the same in your life; go along with the flow, but use your senses, otherwise you will be blind to problems in front of you. Take it easy, but remain aware and alive.

KNOW YOURSELF

Risk being yourself

It is very important that when moving you do not create disruption; leave no victims, no litter, no damage, no structures, no impact. Good movers do not leave anything, good talkers make no mistakes and good totallers recognise the constancy of uncertainty, which is always present and dependable. Don't be scared of it, when it arises around or in you.

The fact that you are a unique individual, and that unique events happen, means you experience different opportunities; these are your chances. If you are a decent human being, you must accept that you will be asked what is behind your well-being. You can explain that you follow nature, but people may be none the wiser about you, because the way they might find out about themselves has limited bearing on you.

This concentration on selfishness produces a remarkable emphasis on detail. This personal knowledge allows humans to be truly selfish. But most surprising and exciting is that you might ever meet anyone who could bear your selfishness and, indeed, even like it. However, this is possible and is the strongest bond. If you are compatible with humans the need for contracts in marriage or business is lessened.

This type of understanding is possible because there is only your law and this cannot be touched by outside agencies, or politicians. Basing things on uncertainty means that you can be comfortable spending time within relationships, jobs, or play, in the knowledge that everything may change; so you can then keep your independence while taking part.

Therefore take care of humans, even the mad and successful; listen to all the things around you and you will re-establish a knowledge of humans and forget the ways of people. A good human has the right qualities and is able to accept his or her bad points. A bad human seems to have the wrong characteristics, but if he/she is honestly bad, you can see this and either avoid or congratulate them for their honesty. Humans honesty is really only part of a good man's character, so they are never bad or capable of premeditation like people.

If you do not listen to yourself you will not learn any lessons. If you are a person who cannot work out why bad things happen, you are either not as bright as you thought, or you are doing things which are against your nature. When you listen to yourself, nothing goes wrong, because that's what you intended. Do something that someone else suggests; it would be puzzling if it went wrong, because you would not know why you did it in the first place. Know yourself and be yourself.

MASTERING
SELF-KNOWLEDGE

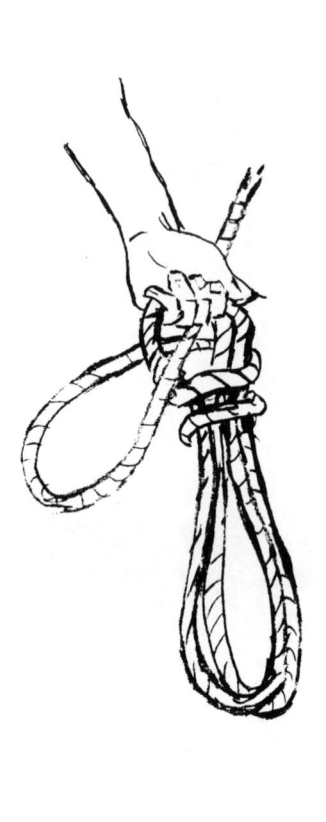

NON-STRIVING

Little effort gives the greatest benefit

The process of discovering an easy life is simple because the ability to change is in your hands, and it takes very little effort to make great strides towards being happy. If you think this is idealistic, ask yourself what would you be, what would you do, where would you go, if there were less image/financial pressures on you? Are your dreams the same as the life you have? Be honest; does this cause you dissatisfaction? Once this emptiness is discovered there is a chance to do something about it. If you can slowly and gently reconcile these differences, the change can be evolutionary rather than revolutionary. By reducing your need for people, riches or reputation (other than that which you will obtain by being yourself anyway,) you will never lose, or be dissatisfied, because you never expected or planned it in the first place.

You will also always have the potential to recreate success again, because you have always done things which were comfortable in the first place. With no ambition or aspiration to acquire that house, that car, that partner, there is less pressure and you will be more likely to obtain not only material and emotional things, but, more importantly, you will obtain them in a form which you truly need. With no constant pressure to have all the things everyone else, or your family, or the media dictates you must have, the desire is removed and so is the need for salesmen, and slowly people will stop trying to interfere with your life. No continuous trying will mean no problems, except of course those which will arise from doing as you wish. You will begin to start living as you are.

SUSTAINABLE

Being comfortable is only visible with time

Living in such an unconsuming way will ensure that you only do things that can be maintained for your lifetime. If you spend all your time concentrating more resources on yourself over and above that which is comfortable, you should not be surprised when you are robbed. How can anyone be surprised by individuals' stealing possessions, if they are not made use of and they appear valuable. There is a way of living without over-collecting.

A useful guideline is to assess your possessions and your future purchases and how these are to be funded. Then consider the importance of each purchase as if you only had half your current income; what would you feel about your material possessions then?

Taking this view allows you to see the attraction of credit in context and realise how vulnerable these acquisitions could make you. Situations are always loaded in some way, and appreciating the cost and the benefit in the context of actions or purchases will enable you to reasonably take on responsibility.

The best thing is to know what you have, what you need and what you want, in human beings, people, the earth and therefore your place in all things. Live in a way which you can maintain and understand the influences which you need to continue being yourself. Doing business on credit is not sustainable; one day you will have to pay it back, and maybe on that day you will not have the resources to do that!

ACCEPTANCE

Can you accept misfortune as well as success?

Central to having a good life is acceptance in all its various forms. Acceptance means being able to be unimportant. To know that the human body is misfortune and the things that happen are a consequence of this. The body is a misfortune because without it you would not need to feed yourself, you would not have hang-ups about the size of your bottom or whether you have met enough of the opposite sex. You would not damage the environment, through your own, or others', actions. Accept and watch to see how events develop. Remove the constant pressure of the marketing and advertisers' dreams. You can be yourself if what you are enticed by is minimised.

When people say they don't know, this is acceptable, but if they are then unwilling to discuss why they don't know, be extremely suspicious. If they do not, or cannot discuss what they mean or want, you have the opportunity to choose. Take, for instance, a child on a bus, telling his father to tie his shoes. Not unreasonable in itself, but the child wanted them tied in a particular way, a double bow at the back of the shoe. The parent impatiently tied them, but incorrectly. The child kept on until the parent took more trouble and tied them the way he was instructed. Who won and who lost? At first you would think the child won hands down and the parent was doomed to a life of slavery.

The parent was the loser, but for a far more fundamental reason. He had not been able to appreciate the importance of the child's request in the first place. The child had also lost, because he had lost the healthy balance of his father's instruction. Gyerek thinks that when the child has the ability to tie his own shoes, he should be allowed to do it anyway he wishes, but in the meantime he should accept the methods of the parent. This then does not cause the parent stress, shows the child the parent's knowledge and encourages the child to learn how to do up his shoes.

As well as children, this example applies to people who don't know what they want. If they are upset by what they receive, they may equally miss out on all that experience and learning. But it is very important that humans communicate that their actions are encouraging people to think for themselves, or people think humans are just being difficult. By operating in this way there is trust; you can like the world and all the things in it as much as yourself; you will know what caring and being cared for, means. If you cannot try this way, then you cannot find balance for yourself.

Conduct yourself fairly during quiet and peaceful times. But remember, however, if there is a battle to fight, wherever it may occur in your life, be unpredictable. Being difficult to understand means you have a brief advantage and may be able to work out others' intentions. By doing this you will also be more likely to accept their position, as the use of random behaviour totally confuses. This unpredictability comes from developing an understanding of, and working with, chaos. To get to know chaos you must take note of those occasions when everything is planned, so carefully that nothing could go wrong, yet things often still do. You can recreate this type of disorder by a simple modification of events, be late, or upset, or something unplanned. How will you know how to use chaos to its best potential in the situation? By looking outwards in these situations, you will see the possibilities for errors while others do not. Ultimately the best measure of how contrived others' judgement is should be based on how much the situation varies from your true and honest evaluation; you can then behave accordingly.

SIMPLICITY

The more basic the better

Contrivances which reduce possibilities are always created by people. Laws reduce the scope for life, but boring as they are, they do reduce danger. Human beings know the law without such structure. Weapons are the consequence of laws and if they are well looked after and maintained, there is always the likelihood of war. But this is not just in nations; it is in people and their thoughts and feelings as well. If people know how to argue, they will. Recognising this gets you through the confusion and distraction everywhere around you, which is created by these organised structures. Acknowledging the reasons for the rules, regulations and behaviour helps remove falsity and you may be able to see those who wish to confuse.

People are horribly clever and the more they push themselves from their nature and their true feelings, the more alien the events which occur. Husbands murder their wives, lovers are violent towards their partners, through sheer jealousy. How bizarre!

It is a fact that the more rules there are, the more likely they are to be broken, because they exist in the first place. Gyerek hopes you could be a quiet and peaceful human being, but there are so many agitated and excited people around that honesty is being forgotten. Being yourself at all cost removes ambiguity and makes you richer.

CALMNESS

Seeing the small things reduces dependence on the big

Learn the flavour, the taste, the joy of doing nothing, as this will increase your awareness in the things you do and the things which happen to you. Take the time you need to recuperate, to rest, and be ready to be active once more and to do this in a way which is comfortable - try to work when you feel like it. This brings a feeling of comfort into all actions and the stress quickly disappears, leaving only the next moment to enjoy.

Remember that when people do not understand honest feelings, they must be given attention. They will probably misunderstand what you have to say. Humans attain pleasure from small events, action, or phenomena. Everything in nature, the universe and the earth seems to work with no effort and superb efficiency, so why should you work hard? Everything is made of small things; by doing these you will achieve the big. Do the small things you *say* and you will taken seriously.

Gyerek attains calmness by being part of the natural world. Swimming up to a mile out to sea, he slowly forgets the entanglements of people. He moves in the water, looking at the sea bed; discovering the plants, and animals. He listens; the sounds; the splashing of the sea, the calls of birds overhead, and the motors of boats far out to sea. He touches the water, and the whole experience touches him. He is respectful, quiet and polite; not wishing to interrupt. No danger from natural surroundings has stopped these encounters, and no harm befalls him. People are scared of nature and never experience it.

People cannot secure this feeling in their minds, they have forgotten that the natural world is the medium which recreates them. It provides their food, shelter, their ability to breed; in fact everything: why is this forgotten.

PERSONAL TREASURE

Mercy, economy and the nerve to let others go first.

The type of life decribed in this book is very attractive, but it seems so easy people do not think it is possible. But it is easy, also easily forgotten, because there are no groups to remind you. This individual understanding is the central balance.

All you really need is the ability to move, the truth, and it is easy to be alive. You have a truth inside you. Listen to it. There are three important things you need to start on the self-discovery trail. The first is mercy. Not the wishy-washy way it is normally seen, but a strong inner understanding which allows for mistakes, misunderstanding and naivety. The second is economy, not the financial cost of things, or money matters, but *eco* which means earth, and *nomy* which means numbers; understanding the connection between money and the resources we need for life and the world around us. Finally, the confidence to dare not to be first. This ability allows you to see others' efforts and not always to want the glory for yourself.

These qualities are lost in people, because they try to be brave, generous and always first - following some kind of hidden rules that say I must do this, I must do that. There is less chance of disagreement, more chance of understanding when individuals have open-minds.

DISCIPLINE

Sticking to what's best for you

Wisdom comes from the type of straightforwardness that is not influenced by distraction, but people love to be side-tracked.

Discipline from distraction such as an audience, fine clothes, fighting, a good meal, more possessions than needed, is easily said and easily done if the consequences of taking are remembered. It is very important to continually use your senses and remind yourself of having no set path. There are always circumstances trying to return you to a limited existence, so remain aware and maintain your flexibility. Having the discipline to retain your way of doing things will maintain your unique potential; doing everyone else's bidding will only make you another member of the grey army, who are starved of character.

But this limiting of character is even more pronounced in resources. For instance, you cannot make the British Isles any bigger, it is just the size it is. Therefore any increase in the amount of land you have is as a result of someone else's loss. This also applies to money. Money is a consequence of resources. Nowhere in nature is a profit expected. If a lion catches and kills an antelope, it does not get any more than the antelope. Imagine that if the lion catches the antelope, it expects a rabbit for its success. It does not sound quite right, does it? So why do people expect more than the return for the service they offer? Because people are naturally greedy of course. This greed in business, emotion, and in all things is the thing which truly sets people away from humans.

Humans know that a fair and honest respectable trade is essential, and Gyerek is not impressed by profit-motivation. Making a good living is different to taking everything. Taking everything means you also receive unnecessary negative things.

GIVING/UNSELFISHNESS

Honest selfishness helps everyone

Humans are able to be themselves without concern about the hidden expectation of people or situations. However, there are of course acceptable means of behaviour, but these are natural to humans, because they observe and are sensitive to different situations. This meeting of your character and people's behaviour is what Gyerek calls the *convergence of infinity*. Infinity is all the possibility, the unlikelihood of the universe existing in the first place and that you could be so happy in your situation, that you would not wish to be anywhere else. Observe this wonder and share it when there are people to listen. The result is that situations are free exchanges and there is no pretence. If this is not possible, something is being hidden and you will know this instantly.

Convergence is the mother of the universe. The uniting of positive and negative forces to form all things, and your life, is the same. Uniting the negative parts of your life with the positive makes for a stunning and wonderful recreation of your personality.

Females or males can make their opposite sex helpless by denying motion (both social or sexual intercourse), and they can also attract by using the same method. Humans know that confidence comes from understanding the power of stillness; can you be still? If you can understand stillness, you will become confident and you will recreate your success. It is also true that if you are small and confident you will understand the insecurities of the big and brutish. This will guarantee eventual success. A growing national economy, or a successful individual, will attract others; humans realise that they must work with the successful, each doing what they should do; the total unity of unselfish and selfish individual needs. This is a fair trade, both giving and receiving. Humans understand this, people just exploit and use.

DEVELOPING
JUDGEMENT

DISPERSAL

Giving out always comes back

Propagation is the method by which nature recreates itself. This happens by dispersal, rather than by the concentration of money and resources which happens when people wish to recreate. Nature works in a dispersive way. In the universe there is a great deal of space, matter and movement. On earth this is also true and there are processes continually taking place to balance the distribution of this space for both the world around us and how we and others work within it. So when you can enjoy sharing, it becomes easier for humans to share with you. You can get on, but this is only possible if you give to start with, and then others will then be more likely to invest in you.

The extent to which these cycles affect you is dependent on the way you move. If you only do the things you need to, you will be troubled with no more than what you expect as part of your normal routine, safe in the knowledge that the universal processes always tend towards balance. So if you have too little, there should be more available from something or someone with too much. This is probably the best explanation of the tendency of people to be aware of the resources of each other prior to breeding.

If the commitment to breed is only based on the acquisition of resources and money, your relationship will only last for a short time, because the only thing you have in common is breeding. Having a financially successful partner does not guarantee the relationship with your partner, or how as parents you will bring up the children; it will just mean you have money. Which would you prefer - an incompetent rich partner, a handsome pauper, or a poor genius?

Gyerek thinks that the best choice depends on the most awareness. There is always plenty of everything, so understand your place in the concentration and dispersal cycle, and be comfortable with what you need, rather than with what you want, and remember, the money might not always be the most helpful or reliable. Look very carefully because there is no ideal partner; the best-looking may have, no conversation, while the best conversation may come from individuals you don't fancy. The interesting thing is that most find a happy medium; and the most important is that you remember yours is the wisest choice, so don't follow the media, follow what you like.

ANTICIPATION

Think about what happens now, not tomorrow or yesterday.

Dispersal may be a start, but the real freedom from certainty can be cultivated by appropriate anticipation. If approached without assumption many problems can be avoided without difficulty.

By being flexible, being concerned with the little things, dispersal can operate in your favour. Deal with things which can influence you before they happen. Anticipation identifies the people and events you should avoid; also the humans and circumstances in which you should participate. All this is possible through feelings. Trusting your direction will lead you into good and bad, but if you don't have the bad you don't get the good either. Whichever you have at the time, good or bad, is better than nothing.

The media is driving us into bubbles of fear. It tells today of how dangerous everything is. Gyerek believes this is nonsense. During the medieval period, only 400 years ago, there were no police, no civil law, and no protection. Killing, rape, mugging, etc were commonplace. Yes, there are dangers today, but they were far worse in the past. There are so few major crimes that they can be considered sensational. So use your senses, participate in safe situations, enjoy this freedom.

The public space that we all use, the tube, the street, exhibitions, etc are relatively safe today, so consider the information the media provides. Anticipation helps us assess the comfortable times to talk, the media kills our willingness to relate to other individuals.

This anticipation must not be an act, or have a vested interest. This skill is associated with things which can harm you, rather than help you go forward. You should also be keenly aware that when anticipating, on the verge of correctly working out the position, you may stop. So give as much thought to the end as to the beginning and you will always be sure. Look for liberty from the need for possessions, costly items, or bigotry. Unnecessary confusion stops things being as they should be and pleasure comes from being confident to talk when you would like to.

SELF RESPECT

Listen to others, but never doubt yourself

Always maintain a respect for your own view in different situations. If you are happy already, this book will probably only have confirmed your conclusions. You are a human and well-equipped to solve difficulties. If, however, you have conflict or confusion, then it's up to you to ultimately solve them, with or without others. Don't depend on anything to do with images.

Depend on your ability, and handle problems with the basic idea that you live your life as an open and honest person. If you are open, why do you have a problem? What's wrong? You or the situation? With this kind of approach no events or problems are insoluble. Know yourself without show, know how to discover all, yet do not say you know everything. This will allow you to be yourself avoiding conflict with other people.

The source of insight is always from deep feelings and if you believe in your feelings you can comfortably live within chaos. Sample these feelings regularly, taste them for a while, like jam contained in a jar, then allow them to go. When moving, do not forget your weaknesses and your appreciation of the enormous beauty all around you. Stay independent and balanced. But when dealing with people, ask yourself; why should I act like everyone else?

To continuously explain being yourself is to lose track. To waste effort is to meet other people's needs, and to lose sight of your own. At the end of the day we all live in a world of people, so be confident and they will notice.

POPULARITY

Risk being yourself; it may upset, it may not

By keeping true to yourself, if you do have conflict with people, there is always the possibility of a lasting aftertaste. So, what is a good solution when it come to problems with people? If you do what you intended without compromising, this is what you wanted to do. If you are then popular it is an easy thing to maintain without effort, because it is you.

If you are not popular then you must accept your lack of appeal, or modify yourself to the circumstances. But remember the more you change, the harder it will be to maintain. The ultimate consequence of doing what others want is the collapse of you or the situation, so be careful. If you always give, no-one will sample your way of living and slowly you will be less alive, affected by the deadening forces of people. You will maintain a level of popularity by removing your own choice. Unconditional giving, whether by choice or habit, threatens everything you hold dear. Firstly, look after your important time, humans, events and things; secondly, look at the expectations of people.

UNBIASED

Keep true to yourself

Problems happen because people always have an interest in what you do. Then there are your friends, and others are humans. People try and give you information which leads you into a position in which you are not comfortable. People feel as if they have given, and gained nothing in return. But most of the time it is your business, and people are making you feel uncomfortable when it is nothing to do with them, so don't be concerned. Sort out who you wish to listen to.

When humans do business they meet their side of the bargain. People are political and try to be involved for other reasons than the task to be completed. Nature is impartial and will always stay with the good, so do not use your new insight and outsight for any other reason than that which arises and needs to be done. In that way you will remain uninfluenced and you will never give more than you can afford.

You should only consider how to employ the surplus of your ability; never lose your unique skills.

GOOD AFTER GOOD

There is no hurt when you care for the thoughts and feelings of others

This type of courage is similar to that of a leader. It takes great attention, and the confidence generated by knowing your own needs, to explain them to others. By always working with your nature, your bad parts will have no strength, because you have described and discussed these, so others can make their minds up about you.

Give time for others to assess their needs, so problems will not be made for the future and there will only be good after good. And even if a situation or relationship ends, you will have always been yourself and not have made promises you could not keep, so there will be no lasting problem.

FORGETTING

Remembering less

When the humans and people around you know what you like there is far less need for words. Wasting effort cannot go on indefinitely. The processess of the earth are efficient by working as they see fit. The rain, the sunshine, the snow can last for a short or long time, for as long as the conditions are correct there is no stress. So if nature, the universe, the earth cannot always work consistently, how do you think you can?

When you become comfortable with the person you are, the situations and the people around you, you are accepted. So learn who you are and then forget and learn again.

SEEING

Seeing through the mist

In the same way that your conscious thinking and feeling needs to know before you forget, the rest of your subconscious character, the earth and everything else will be recreating and destroying. The universe will be expanding and contracting, nature will be positive and negative. But what is most important is how much of this is visible to you.

To see nature is to acknowledge the weak, to be strong; to realise you are as dependent on the world as a fish is dependent on water. This is for you to know and to use. Sit comfortably in this understanding, but do not challenge others to make them view themselves.

Have you ever taken a walk, in a place you know, when there is a dense fog? You stroll, usually along a path, because you can't see very well, and have a sense of apprehension. The last time Gyerek did this, he followed the path to the top of a hill. Getting higher, all that could be seen were the slopes falling away from the path. The visibility could only have been 40ft. He continued up and when he reached the top, he could only see whiteness all around him, in every direction.

The only feature he could see was a small building in the centre on the hill. If another had taken the same trip they would not have had any idea of the size of the hill, or indeed if there was a view. But Gyerek had been there before and could still picture, quite clearly in his mind, the tremendous view which would have been possible on a clear day. Gyerek had not remembered the view, but it was apparent. This is how most of us experience life; we can see very little because, in the case of life, it is image which forms the mist. Use your senses, your mind, your feelings, observe, ask yourself and others questions, and see beyond the mist.

ON BEING REAL

Bringing it all together

Distraction is everywhere. To participate fully and to be flexible could be a constant effort. To know yourself is very difficult unless you make it easy for yourself by staying in touch with your concerns, rather than trying to pass them to something, or someone else, to handle.

Can you display childish emotion? Can you look into your heart and re-evaluate yourself; be open with people around you? Can you be comfortable with no guidance, no support, no images of religion, science, magicians, or fools? Can you be outside these accepted norms? Remove that suit at work, those Ray Bans on the beach, that ideal partner, that ideal answer, etc. Can you reproduce yourself (have children) to see your own character in your child? Can you decide how you do business, both financially and emotionally? Can you be courageous enough to say 'I want to be me'? Can you move in the way you want without prejudice to yourself or others? Can you be a decent human being? Are you different to people who consume? Too many are consumers.

Do you wish to be part of the things around you and enjoy everything equally well? If you do wish to have such an easier life read on with an open mind. If you do not wish to take responsibility, to learn to modify circumstances to stop those disappointments, you never will be comfortable. It is your choice, no-one else's. If you cannot choose for yourself, don't be angry when humans choose honestly for both you and themselves.

FEELINGS

There is always conflict

Large volumes of information can lead to confusion; your eyes, ears and tastes are deadened. This type of excitement is over-bearing and this type of constant influence can lead you astray. Your feelings are real. Trust them. They are your friends and allies, your support and your future as an individual.

Let go of comfortable fears (the customs, the beliefs, the thoughts, the concerns) and hold on to your intentions. Learn to live and not to hide.

REPETITION

Bringing clarity to your feelings

Balance comes from knowing that all things come from nature. This cannot be said enough as it is easily forgotten. Even the totallers may never discover this truth, because of the diverse ways we all live today.

If you are not happy, move to recreate the conditions which you are happy with (remember nothing is created or destroyed, just changed). Just do it, be yourself for once. It also makes being yourself a second, third, fourth time so easy. When you have the skill to recognise and return to your concerns life is easy. It will nourish, protect, recreate and guide as long as images do not interfere.

RECOGNISING SUBSTANCE

ID

Few of us know ourselves completely

We live with ourselves 24-hours a day, yet very few people are aware of who they are. The Id is the subconscious, the deep thoughts and feelings that influence our attitudes. The surface character, we cultivate is comfortable. A little deeper, into our character however, we begin to worry. Even deeper we become scared. If you do not, or cannot face these even deeper parts, if you cannot know yourself, who else would want to know you?

People prefer the surface; it is like being in a boat in the sea and feeling a sense of safety floating apart from the water. In Gyerek's opinion being in the boat is the dangerous place, because people feel secure, when they clearly are not. Your personality is the same; being on the surface may seem safe, but there are equally great depths which are just below the surface. The sea is a safe place to swim and to dive down into if you take care and use your senses, and your character can be equally safe.

Being apart from nature is artificially comforting, but nature holds the secret to an easy life. Which do you want - swimming with dolphins or driving a speedboat? But remember dolphins keep going after the petrol tank is empty and you don't need a boat to meet them, you just need to know how to swim. So learn to move in your surroundings and you can have natural experiences.

To see inside yourself where no one else can, and say 'I like me', is worth all the effort.

TOTALLERS

Making it all add up

To have enough conviction to know there is no rigid position, is to become proper in different situations. You are able to adapt and become knowledgeable of others' needs, whether they know them themselves or not. There are many potential humans. Most individuals however, wish to be people and will do anything not to be themselves. Don't trouble yourself with that, because they will never be themselves as long as they are flippant. People take notice when you are lively and well; collecting information, rather than possession, to meet your needs? Humans obtain answers from information because they make the sum easier for themselves, by being honest.

Use your insight and outsight. Know it. Feel it. Find a total. Do this slowly, be still, listen, smell, touch, taste, see, feel, think and ask what, when, which, why and how. Then *do* and be still again. Look at what is in front of you and not what you make up for yourself. This is how you can be aware.

EXTERNALITIES

Recognise the worst and never be shocked

Gyerek thinks that during life, three out of ten exist, three out of ten complain about the lack of their ability to exist, and three out of ten just pass from birth to death and survive. Where does the other one reside? It is the human who wants to live.

People do not consider the costs of their actions, so it always seems as if they are getting something, without incurring all the costs. But the cost is unreality. People place distraction into their lives, like shopping etc, as they have few things of substance. If you know yourself, you can travel, face challenges, take on problems and there will be no shock, no injury or crevices for any of the bad to cling to. This will provide you with the ability to assess others' damage, because you cause little yourself. With this skill you can choose to reduce the effects of others on your life.

Why is this possible? Because the forces that numb and deaden self knowledge are unable to take a hold when you are always aware of them. There is no fear, as you have the knowledge of weakness and defeat already.

EVERYTHING IN ALL OF US

You can be yourself, all you have to do is try

With the complete knowledge of using your senses and noticing the subtle in situations, you can understand the whole world. But even without using your senses you can have an inbuilt understanding of the universe. If you cannot use your senses, you will not get a clearer view by travelling the world. You are a snapshot of the whole of existence. All the forces of the universe unite in and all around you. All these simple natural rules exist in everything from our behaviour, to the existence of the largest star in the universe, down to the parts of the smallest atom.

Thinking without the restrictions of scale brings the possibility of explaining the world around you, in the same simple terms as Gyerek relates his comments to the way in which we make our lives easier. Time and space merely describe movement, and movement explains how people live. Unite with this principle and be freed from the falsity of image once and for all.

The more you have to see, the more confusion, the more wasted effort, the more limits. You can know by not travelling, you can evaluate without testing, you can find a balance without striving; without effort means that which comes easily. Add to this a degree of investigation through testing, and you will formulate a true balance.

ONLY NATURE

Why fathom who you are? Just be what you do and feel

Most people spend huge amounts of time, effort, and money on an external image. But only your internal substance is necessary. You may find it difficult to find, but most certainly there is a quite independent essence inside all of us, which all image tries to remove through standardising everything.

By accepting the certainty of uncertainty, you can recognise the constant balance of chaos and control, and by working within this you will see that you can be comfortable with accepting different situations for what they are.

Images make us dress the same, act the same, have the same religion, the same, the same, the same!!! Nature existed long before man evolved, or moved here, and recreates differences between individuals; and everything in the universe. Do not lose the feeling. Sense it, be aware of it, things are because they are, don't forget it and there will be no danger.

CONVERGENCE

It is possible to be yourself and fit in

Do people leave others in ignorance to ensure their power? Of Course not everyone has their own agenda, but people think about helping themselves, and usually at the expense of others. If people could lead by doing what they feel, they would be more like leaders.

They would not consume and would be more like humans. If you lead by observing the wishes of the others, you will never be removed from office, you will be doing their bidding and they will ensure your safety within their group. If you do this the followers will like your judgement, because they do not feel you are invading them.

There is a choice to consume, or to sustain. Good business maintains customers, materials, tools, and colleagues. As long as this feeling is strong, all is possible. It must be remembered that how you approach the universe reflects the way it will affect you.

It is the way that the universe has unfolded which has brought you to the time and place you are today. This is remarkable in itself, but for you to actually enjoy this as well is stunning.

CONTENTMENT

Is not having to know

Knowing that an individual's nature is unique feelings and thoughts is easy to understand, but only humans acknowledge and use it (and even they need help sometimes). Gyerek thinks that forgetting the importance of nature explains the problems of civilisations. He carefully acts in a way which meets his own needs. Once you are comfortable with a singular united way of living, you then only have to go about your daily life; there is no need for energy to be wasted on searching for answers.

Because people do not understand this, they cannot understand Gyerek. They think him strange, but in fact it is they who are not part of all things; they who lead unnatural lives. Humans are rare, because consumers, the people whose lives are constructed around targets of success, that car, that partner, are today rewarded. Some of the abusers of nature are the pilots of industry and are held high. Therefore, if you choose a decent human path for yourself, do not *expect* the honours attached to material success.

The reward you gain is a jewel in your heart; be content that you know, but also remember that, although knowing yourself and your talents, you may fit better into the material world and get rewards anyway.

REMEMBERING

Balance is being able to say no to your vices whenever you like

Have you the discipline to remember where you come from, when shops have so many lovely things? Air, earth, water and fire form the elements, of which you are a part. That cannot be changed, that and these are your rewards. When you move you run with the wind, when you stop, you are firm like the earth; when you dive you are surrounded by a friend in water; when you need defence, depend on fire. It is the hunter who is at one with his surroundings; he enjoys the way he relates to his territory. People who are scared of living in their surroundings dislike the rain and the cold. The hunter enjoys the woods and makes his life within those surroundings.

To believe there is a God which is good, and a devil which is bad, is to believe in image. This breaks the thread of nature, and replaces natural living with manufactured ideas. There is no need for such unproven explanations when the reasons for existence are simple and all around us everyday.

Each person who believes in a God creates god in the most palatable form to them, in their own head. Nature, however, is bigger than any image you can create for yourself, as it is outside your head. If you have no guide, no image and consider just that which is in front of you, no beginning, no end, you will stay keenly in the present. Always remember, and you will maintain your understanding.

KNOWING WHAT TO AVOID

Reach for things that are within your grasp

Knowing what to avoid allows you to keep nature in your memory with all its uncertainty, but this uncertainty is acceptable if you enjoy what you are doing and do not wish to know what the future will bring. Have a challenge, but only one in which you can be successful by being yourself. Overworking or maintaining an image is not truthful, will not last, and at some point will show, or you will become tired of it.

Express yourself, produce a valuable role or service, or just enjoy an interest and your daily work, without exhibitionism. By doing this you will reduce the amount of pressure you place on yourself, which will reduce the baggage of tasks that deaden your brain; you will then be able to think, feel and use your senses. This may even be for the first time.

If you are good, you do not need to do anything other than you can do already, so just continue. Other human beings will know. Over-confidence in an unpredictable universe is foolish. It may seem important to people to be above it all, to overcome, predict and give certainty to people's lives. But this is against the principles of existence itself, so humans see this constant guarantee from people in work, emotion and in all your life as idealistic. Believing in certainty makes Gyerek scared, as it is just an illusion. So make the mistakes and work with the humans you like. Concentrating on talking reduces action. So only say what is necessary and give time to doing. If you do succeed, you will only do it a few times. Do not dwell on your own success, as you will become lazy and miss all the new adventures just around the corner. Do and move. Be a non-consumer and all this excess baggage will be avoided.

STOP SEARCHING

Things are fundamentally very small and untouchable

If human beings could understand nature and the elements, all things would join willingly and naturally obey. The universe and humanity would be one, and calm would affect all things. There would no longer be the need for teaching, or a spoken direction or a view of what to do. Things would just happen. We have to realise that some processes in the universe are just so big that it is nonsense to think we can influence them. By constantly trying to overcome these enormities, we miss the opportunities we do have. Yes, we can build flying machines. Yes, we will probably learn how to travel through the universe, but we should learn to do these things by using the methods which already exist in the universe. We make the most efficient cars by making them stream-lined like fish and birds. Wake up from crass techno-solutions; look at nature, see how the objects which move in the universe and in molecules can cross their space. You do not have to look further than your own nose. You just have to make the commitment to be aware; to observe the phenomena, and then be open-minded; to appreciate it.

Educated people divide the universe. They break things down and give them names in the hope they may understand them. But naming and scientific testing have not explained things and never will because they have a fundamental flaw. If you name a thing and test for it in a man-made and clockwork world you will always find it, because you invented it. But nature is neither clockwork or man-made.

Science seeks to explain nature, but along the way its systems of enquiry have become distant from the beautiful and uncertain natural systems which scientists wish to measure. Mankind can no longer use its large brain to applying rigid scientific methods to nature, as these tests miss the majority of the processes at work. Science makes its greatest observation when it is naive. Newton watched an apple fall. That was his inspiration. Science today could learn a good lesson from Newton. Science has forgotten that it should understand nature before applying its discoveries. Being appropriate when we come to large technological modifications to the way we live would avoid later problems. For instance, nuclear power is not necessarily bad; it is only so because people did not work out how to stop it, before they started. Nature is nature. Stopping searching and starting listening is the way to work with it.

THE BOTTOM LINE

Everything depends on movement

Water is the principle element because it underpins all life. Therefore anything which can behave like water will be best - the most fluid and flowing. If you can take the path of least resistance, you can be effective at moving and creating a change in your life, like a river carves its valley shape. When you hit a rock, be deflected rather than halted. Flow around, or over, and take a new path. Don't be concerned by the obstacles, the bad experiences, relationships, or work, just rub against them and then flow on.

This is most palatable, because you give what is wanted and no more. This is fine, as long as it is what you can afford. You will stand for honesty and you will be supported in return. Trusting nature, yourself and those who trust you, will mean that you will be outside politics. No political sabotage will befall you.

MAINTAINING UNDERSTANDING

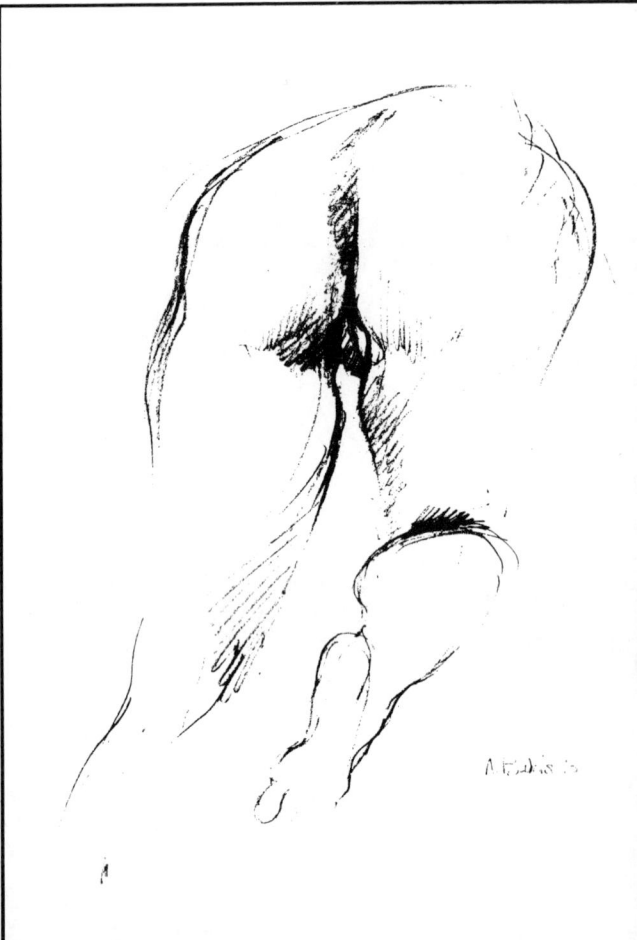

DIFFERENCES

Just look without bias and see the difference

If you wish to solve your troubles, stop looking for answers. Must you always think? Must you have some framework like science, religion, societies, time-planners, magic to make your worries? Just eat and be merry; go and see some beauty in the countryside.

Drift in a different location for a while. Look at information and soak it up like a baby does before it can talk, and do not expect friends or answers. There are so many consumers and very few individuals who can just be. People are organised, and thinking. Gyerek is foolish and emotional, Gyerek is quiet and small. He tries to understand the way things are, rather than suggesting artificial mathematical representations of nature, which is the current trend. Real visible events move Gyerek towards nature, like he is in a boat on a river drifting along without a rudder, but always moving in a way which will lead to an easy life, the same way the river follows its natural course. People are busy. They are within limits of time and effort. Gyerek has no limits; he listens to his nature for success.

DESIRE AND DISCONTENTMENT

Reduce the things you think you need

When nature is understood, the resources around us are utilised to humans' benefit. The land is farmed well, the population lives within the resources. Resources are recreated by nature and are there for individuals to turn to (if they have access to them) in times of difficulty. Nature works at its speed and it has times of disaster as well as harvest. When this is forgotten, resources are used incorrectly. The land is abused, burnt and there is war; the population dies. This abuse create wants; and wanting leads to a belief in the possibility of creation. Just wish it and it is possible! Ever more resources for ever more consumption! This falsity has attracted and confused the development of the human race for centuries. To be rid of it makes you look at the advantages of what you have, rather than what you wish for.

People believe that if they ask an image to solve all their biological, material, and emotional wants, there is a possibility they may be solved. This only leads to awful dissatisfaction. This misunderstanding is greed.

Balance comes from the things which are really important, such as feeding your children, having a roof to shelter under etc. Know what you have, know when you have enough.

OBSESSION

Recognise your persistent behaviour

We all have regular behaviour which is as predictable as the earth travelling around the sun. What is a mystery to most is whether this can be made obvious, like the earth's movement. You must use your senses, not only to see how your surroundings work, but also yourself. The sun, like our understanding of our character, seems a long way off. Scientists use special telescopes to allow them to observe the sun. The sun is too bright to get any information; by using a black circle at the centre of the telescope they can see what happens around the outside. You also need some way of blotting out the brightness of the rest of your life to look more closely at the way you regularly react.

You cannot simply place a black circle over a lens, like the telescope. But you do need to blot out some of the distractions, to effortlessly watch the way you behave. This enables you to recognise how you move and to be aware of how your obsessive behaviour can be avoided.

Contented human beings never have disappointment, they only have the lows which are the necessary opposites of the highs. If you are honest about your regular behaviour, it just becomes another part of your character, there when you need it.

POLITICS

Choose honesty or politics

If you cannot accept that you have obsessions, the politicians will. Politicians does not just mean party politics, (eg in the UK Conservative, Labour etc) it also means any individual offering deals to meet your needs. Being yourself has no vested interest, it is just you. Being someone else's person only leaves you trying to do others' objectives and this is obvious and acceptable, if it is suits you as well. Following your own interests has no time scale so there are no deadlines; being constantly active produces many more tasks to complete. When human beings offer help, they find out what is required and help completely. People don't listen, and then leave many things to do. Bullies don't even try and convince, they force. All of these confusions are born out of the politics, yet curiously if you choose honesty as a guide you will be better placed to understand the efforts of politicians.

Politics arises when nature is forgotten. The individual first has strength in his/her actions, which will be judged by their peers. If their opinion does not cause his behaviour to modify towards the constructed 'norms' judgement will be decided in the courts, which may lead to punishment. This political enforcement was designed to stop dangerous behaviour, but in fact it reduces individual expression, and the more pressure and civil laws the less freedom.

What is important is to remove politics, as this is just a further image. Look behind the discussion to see the substance. If this substance is not described simply and carefully so that it can be understood by the population, at best this type of leadership should not be trusted and at worst should be called downright lying. If leaders are unable to explain their actions simply, they should not be trying to convince you of anything.

Be concerned with the substance, not the glitter, and choose completely. Do not accept anything less. Salesmen (which certainly includes politicians) take advantage of people's needs and desires. There are plenty of people who will encourage salesmen, if it is in their interest to do so.

Gyerek would like to suggest an honest system of government, which is based on democracy. It would benefit the country as a whole, rather than political leaders or industrialists. The geographic distribution of boundaries would be based on random selection, to give an appropriate number of MPs, for instance 650 in the UK. All MPs should represent their district, being individuals with no political party affiliation. All issues should be voted on by MPs, and decided by majority; with MPs being made aware that decisions would be made by referendum, if settlement was not arrived at.

This system would recognise that there is always a tendency for some individuals to try and lobby; to create group voting. So voting ethics would initially encourage MPs to vote with their consciences. If the organised lobbying continued, enforcement to stopping the practise would follow. Officials would be fairly elected, by a majority of voting MPs. Their performance and promotion could then be decided upon by the country, rather than by political party. No affiliation to organised groups, such as sponsors, committees, societies etc, would be allowed during office. This would be rewarded by one set payment to reflect their importance to the country. If necessary, an independent audit of the MP's accounts would ensure that no further payments were received.

The complete and honest answering of questions would be encouraged, without fudging or evading questions, resulting in re-election of the official concerned. This honesty would be strictly enforced. The largest political organisation would be a company with no government representation. When Gyerek was young his mother said, 'if you don't tell the truth, I cannot help you'. The only time a child is tempted to lie is when he is embarrassed, has something to hide, or is being silly. A country cannot be helped when its officials behave as misguided children. The government system described only encourages honesty; why can't we have it? Gyerek is sure there is no decent reason why we shouldn't. People would argue they have a lot to lose. But if they gained by being dishonest, they shouldn't have gained in the first place.

There is no issue too great for a country's population to voice opinion, if they are given an honest choice.

JOINING

Link all your thoughts and feelings

All is from one seed, and nature knows when it is whole. Space is complete when empty (space is where there is nothing), earth is complete when solid (earth is when there is something firm), feelings are full when they have substance and gentleness (feelings are when there is emotion, inside motion), the valley is complete when filled with a river, all things are alive because not a single part of a single atom is still, and has the tenacity to recreate itself. Knowing when things are real enables you to identify fakes. This is an invaluable skill and produces the kind of awareness required to exploit your nature and your surroundings in an appropriate way.

It is not the politicians that unite, it is the attractions of nature. Nature provides space, earth, feelings, the valley, the country, the individuals and all other things; political groups then try to organise. Their efforts are always to detriment of the resource.

Have concern for all things, but understand that to please yourself, you have to know who you are. Image may teach you a small part of what is opposite of image, but the real test is the need not to preach. Once you know who you are you realise, from those still struggling around you, that you have joined nature.

CONSENSUS AND THE PEOPLE

There is a universal truth

Now you are really beginning to explore nature you can discover what happens when you forget it. The true result is that you begin to be interfered with. Things begin to re-influence you, the thinking returns and you go back to the pretence of hiding.

This returning to the unreal is useful because it highlights the vision and insight which following nature brings. You are able to communicate in both worlds and understand your place in them. Truth begins to disappear because of the influence of people, and the need to organise the family and friends to stop manipulation becomes apparent. If there is no trust in society, the need for image becomes clear. But image never solved anything and never will; when will people realise this?

SPOILT EASILY

Protect your potential, but don't spend all your time doing it

This honest way of life can easily be lost and the need for images means that you are not living honestly already. No image can save the universe, because image is not the force which recreates existence. You cannot improve what exists in the universe and image cannot improve your life, because it has no substance.

If you use image to try and change, you will merely recreate agitation. Try and keep your nature by holding it close. Lots of events will try to influence that, but be balanced and avoid self-satisfaction and you will have a better chance of being a decent human being.

LOST CONTROL AGAIN

Be comfortable about knowing the process of nature without symbols

To develop balance, remove the baggage; this will be achieved by doing nothing and seeing what you need and what you don't. But when you are fed-up with knowing yourself, just lose yourself for a while. Don't panic - all the work and understanding involved in finding yourself will not disappear; you will just give it a rest. When you feel comfortable again, all your understanding will flood back to its normal place.

These rests are essential and will give the relaxation required to be ready to wonder again about the nature of things. It is acceptable to lose balance because you are rubbing off the excesses of what you need to live. Let the process continue; you cannot control it by being clever.

CHECKING

Watch yourself doing

While you are letting go of thinking and understanding your feelings, keep checking to make sure you know where you are in the world of people. The universe recreates. The mother carries the child, and in the same way reproduction is at the centre of the universe and is the condition which gives rise to all things. To know this condition is to know the processes, illustrated by the expression; like mother like child.

Knowing that the universe is dependent on nature, that processes and features are a result of this recreation, brings the acceptance that at the centre of the universe there are cycles. Knowledge of this gives rise to quiet discovery. Keeping aware without speaking in this world gives knowledge, but the noisy and busy world of people blots out investigation and appreciation and there is nothing to see. By discovering the small things, you learn when to be gentle; use your senses to check your inner views. This is how you keep in touch with what's around you and are safe from harm.

APPLYING THE TRUTH

PEACE

Saving yourself is possible by doing your small things

If the leaders could realise that there is a need for us to achieve our potential, and would produce a framework for all things to be what they are, nature would develop in peace. If you, or the leaders, then wished to do things, they would make simple constructions.

These structures would not encourage aspiration, and without aspiration there is a gentle peace. With peace there are no battles, no requirements and no problems which nature cannot overcome. With this kind of peace it is easy to understand the agitation around you, and minimise its effect on you. The battles you are then faced with are those you can potentially win, so there is always the chance luck may smile on you.

There are battles however; why should you want everything on a plate? Some battles have to be fought anyway, and are necessary for you to be yourself. Your friends, family and other humans are worth assisting.

TAILOR-MADE

Everyone knows best for themselves

Humans see nature as a joy; it is only people who are scared or inconvenienced by the elements, the rain, the emotions of others. People want protection. To say you like nature can gain allegiance, and other human beings may be influenced. But their attention will only be gained by brave and skillful actions. These actions may be difficult for unsure humans, but sometimes it's worth waiting for humans to find themselves before they can be real. When the time is right they will be there; just be there with your nature. You have your own unique way of working; by using time wisely you can work towards living in your chosen way.

The journey to find your nature is as short, or as long as you are from thoughts and feelings now. When you are at one with your nature, you are at one with the earth, the universe, and nature itself. You will achieve everything within your potential, everything you deserve. If you are not a human, don't be surprised, saddened or overjoyed. It is the way you are. The success is that you started and completed the journey to the centre of the universe. It is your nature and the nature of all things that you have found. It is with this knowledge that you can start to live rather than just surviving; being happy, rather than just drifting. You now have the ability to recognise yourself and to see more of the things around you.

LIKE THE GRASS

Bend and move with the situations in which you find yourself

With this knowledge of yourself, you are confident to rise and fall like the grass. To and fro, nothing to everything. Give up and start again, go back to nothing to gain all. To know that desire causes choice, and this leads to confusion. Always think of yourself; you have taken some effort to discover this and now you know yourself and what others are looking for. By knowing that you do not have to take command of situations, you will have a confidence which is attractive, which will filter into all your dealings. If you are being watched, rather than doing the watching, you will have the edge and extra decision-making time to help you achieve what you enjoy.

If you feel something is unusual, it probably is. If you think about that feeling you will recognise how or why it came about. Making no excuses makes you different. No wasted effort means that you are efficient and you will be judged on your actions. No promises means only proper reactions. No arguing brings only consensus. These are conclusions with substance. Knowing strengths and weaknesses, you will gain the time you need to develop the space in which you need to live.

GENTLE

Take care out there

There are few rules and few complications for human beings. Only people need rules, so that they can cheat. Fortune comes out of your understanding of misery and carrying that with you will enable you always to see where there is happiness. Nobody knows the future, because there is no clear calendar, but really would any of us like to know exactly what was going to happen to us in the next hour, let alone the next few days? Be open to events and impatient to problems. This will help you to recognise and solve them more quickly. In the long run, this is always better for you.

Moral excellence is a magical insight which comes from the ability to feel completely and not censor unless you need to. People's lack of acceptance of this quality from within is a great problem, so try to stay pointed, without cutting. Cutting without wounding, by being open and honest within bounds. Be striking and talented without robbing the judgement of others. Leave others to find out for themselves, but they may obviously learn from you if they are able.

APPRECIATION

Being perceptive prepares you for movement

Why do people resign themselves to meaningless lives, never being able to fulfil their potential? Gyerek thinks that it's because some individuals have that nature. In some other cases the government and other leaders wish the best things for themselves, taking opportunities from you.

This therefore reduces the chances for individuals to develop their way of moving. By anticipating, you will read these intentions early so you have time to check before your opportunity is removed. This will provide a better chance of seeing the opportunity in the first place, as well as being able to exploit it. The law is now used to produce the framework for an individual's potential.

There are too many laws, causing unrest and ultimately anger. There is little time within the laws and rules to spend time on anything other than paid work, therefore people stay thoughtless.

If there is no thought, how are you to fully understand and appreciate life? Living with small things which are easily within your means allows you to have a greater appreciation of your life, the earth and the universe. It is possible to give value to activities which involve self-satisfaction through your nature, if you know what you enjoy.

FREEDOM

Don't be worried by the downs

If you are not worried by having small things, people lose the power to tempt you. If a law is so great that it takes away the freedom to be the decent human you have discovered, then there may be risks to be taken to ensure that freedom. You must be willing to challenge these laws if you feel they prevent you from being real. Just because people make laws, does it mean they are correct for you or that you have to live by them to the letter? You can move, remember, you can see if there are places better suited to you, or use the free things - water, air, and fire, or friends, to help you.

If you are to have any successes there must be challenges and disappointments, so accept them as part of the puzzle. Do this, and you will be free from losses and disappointments because you will understand they are all part of participating. You can then be a happier participant.

The land unfortunately has many restrictions; it is difficult to imagine how everyone can live, rather than just survive, in the world people have created, if they have no access to the land. But you must try and keep moving. Do not be anything you are not, and all will be well.

LIVING

Want all experiences

Living as you are keeps you young. Mental and emotional youth is a great irritant to people who have given up, because it shows them they have stopped. Young growth is always tender in nature, in plants, animals, new features of the earth, and all things. This newness in humans is their hope. Individuals who are young at heart keep their hope, and have the best opportunity of finding a better way of living and being real.

If you have given up the possibility of being yourself, you have already died. If something is filled; plants by sap, hills by rock and humans by hope, then there is no withering and death. If you are not young, you become old like people, stiff, strict and with lost potential. Gentleness is in movement; there is no stopping its great flexibility. The people, those who are unyielding, will not last and the movement of humans will cause this stiffness to disappear.

GIVING GUIDANCE

Be very careful when thinking of helping others

The force of this movement is fluid like water; it stops without injury, it cuts without damage; it has no equal. It goes where no larger forces can go, it overcomes stiffness without trying. Everyone knows that water and the hope of humans are unstoppable, but few are guided by this substance. If you are guided by this force, you will meet others like yourself, you will be most likely to do all the things you wish to and, most important - even if you fail you will have been doing what you enjoy.

By being part of your nature and that of other humans, it is possible to see how both you and events shape themselves and then have a role within them. Nature supports disaster; it is part of the way of all things, but to people this is not an attractive concept. But this is the real illustration of polarity, and in fact if difficult things did not occur, we would be far less able to handle them, less able to see good parts of our lives, and less real as a consequence.

WINNING

True success has no consequence

Nature hates threats, as it never threatens; it just gets on with being itself. Wise men recognise this and prefer the weak. Only aggressive men prefer the strong. To win, wise men use different tools and only use weapons when there is no other choice. Peace and quiet are the important things.

Nature is peaceful; how much lasting peace do the images of religion, politics, science or other beliefs bring? Very little if any. They just cause agitation, dissatisfaction and wars. So do you believe in the super-natures of all controlling gods, technology and people, or the hope and truth of your own and the nature of the universe?

Believing in yourself has two great benefits; firstly it is right for you; secondly, if there are gods, they made you the way you are. Being yourself is to do what they intended. So there is no need to listen to earthly influences telling you what they intended. Understand this and nothing can go wrong. Science, religion, politics or foolishness can be part of life, to a lesser or greater extent, they all struggle to create a theory of life, but it's for you to decide how useful they are.

Do you like killing? There is a difference between how nature and people approach this. Nature just does what it does. People create wars. These produce defeat for a group or individual. In nature, animals kill to survive and there is no song and dance. People, under the banner of civilisation, try and explain the politics of conflict, but are still only killing to gain access areas from which they can then derive food; they also kill to eat, but are dishonest in their explanation. War (and any laws securing rights to resources) results in limited resources for some, if this process is very visible. Some have all the resources, and give hand-outs to the other people to keep them passive, such as in the UK. This managed access to resources further reduces the ability of individuals to fulfil their potential and ensures a future for the owners of the resources. In humans the aim is to be themselves and to do what they feel happy doing and to live and let live, and be happy. This would seem to be completely incompatible to the activities of people. Who are you? A person, or human? The leaders of people are apart from the majority, their sorrow is observing the effects of their actions. Humanity loses. Why is all this necessary? If there were sense, there would be some show of weakness, some acceptance of responsibility, but often there is none.

FULFILMENT

Understand that you need no more than a full belly and an empty mind

If you believe in nature in this form, people will think you are foolish. Foolishness is trying to be something you are not (if you are foolish, that is what you are, don't be concerned by it unless you wish to be). If you do what you can do, you will do something good for yourself. Observe polarity - all of the ups and downs, ins and outs, losses and gains, with the same enjoyment. They are all part of life. The work of people is part of a human's life. Nature will always underlie events; act on whatever is your nature.

If however you wish to be your nature, there are serious emotional consequences. These will be the most freeing, risky, exciting and consistent. Gyerek cannot offer the solution to issues affecting each one of you; he can however offer the solution which suits him. If people cannot face a large amount of your actions, you are not in the correct situation.

If however you are very happy in your situation and it may only be one part of your character which threatens your complete happiness, you would be wise to consider hiding this characteristic very well. If this action becomes more than just a distraction, however, it must be admitted and accepted for the benefit of all.

This will then allow the others to make up their minds. To help, you must remember how immunisation works. An injection puts a mild form of the disease into the blood and then the body's immune system is able to create antibodies to hold off the full disease. If you place a small problem in a situation a solution is created in the same way. So at some time you will have to make an emotional commitment, but to what extent must be discussed and lived with on an ongoing basis.

Commitments come in many forms, as many as there are people to make them. It is becoming increasingly obvious that both humans and people do not fit into the contracts: marriages, promises, ideas of relationships.

What's wrong with making up your mind as you go along; everyone knows that you don't know what will happen in the future, so how can you promise anything? It is not intended that you exploit others' feelings, though people do find this easy; the intention is that individuals appreciate that things change, and should not be concerned by this, even within deep feelings.

APPLYING THESE IDEAS

Think only when you need to

If you need to think, things are not usually as they should be to make you happy. The thoughts which are then produced cloud emotional enjoyment. If you say 'I Don't Know', you should not be upset if others make your mind up for you. You cannot live life in such a blind and unresponsive way; you have to make choices even if by doing so you might lose something important. Decide what mean the most and enjoy them. Look after these things and the others' which are not needed will reduce in importance and slowly disappear.

Thoughts which you need help with lead to a dependency on others organisational thinking. You have stopped feeling, and now believe that thinking can solve your problems. In the end a shrink will only tell you to trust yourself anyway. Your nature makes no effort to solve problems; you just stop thinking and start listening and feeling.

DOING NOTHING ALLOWS FOR EVERYTHING

Give time to let things just happen

Nature will develop through disruption as well as calm, so do not remove the importance of problems. Allow for events to take their course and just do your best.

This will allow for possibility instead of just living in a controlled bubble. Do not restrict yourself to one type of life; try everything and regularly remind yourself of how far off-balance you are.

If objections to your aims are encountered, it will probably be for one of the following reasons; jealousy, lack of interest, misunderstanding, or a vested interest. Learn and do on and then go on. This removes complication and dissatisfaction. The true battle is to defeat the forces which stop you from doing your things. You can go against nature only for a short time so choose well, or just do what you always feel.

LEARNING

Awareness is not specifically taught

Death can be ugly; so can life. That is how it is and should be. There is no point disbelieving or arguing about it. Gyerek cannot persuade you of anything and he would not like to try. Others try to persuade you, and you will try to persuade others. No end of suggestion will give a better chance for you to be happy, unless you are open-minded and willing to take on new ideas and feelings. Gyerek wishes that you open up in time to enjoy yourself. If you are not scared of collecting information, you can just follow the path of least resistance and will find the easiest way to live.

The words you use are too often not your own, but are someone else's.

Listen to all things and the answer will be found in nature every time. There is no need to collect ideas, people or possessions above those which you need to move. The more you participate, the more achievements will result and they will be to your liking. These will, like all nature, expand to fit the available space or time you have. Nature is the centre. Work with it.

UNTHREATENING

Allowing for others

So how is it possible to work with nature, yet ignore people? If there is no influence from people there is no competition. If there is no competition there is no urgency. If there is no urgency there is no restriction. If there is no restriction there is no want. If there is no want there is no resistance and no images. Doing is the important thing, living in a sustainable and happy way rather than being defensive. People try and place limits on you, and how you handle these will determine how close to nature you will become.

People place limits on their lives, so that they can live them within their own comfortable constraints. So do not propose solutions for people, unless you are sure they are ready for totalling. See the individual in front of you, not the one you would like to see, and do not scare them.

IDENTIFYING SUCCESS

WRITING IS OVER

If you believe something, do something

It is sensible to meet others and remember all your own needs and wants at the same time. Fighting at any time is bad, but especially when you are in a new situation. You don't have to explain, all the time, the thoughts and feelings you have and how you will ultimately react. But when all the feelings, thoughts and observations lead to action, only a fool would not react.

This requires confidence and the ability to listen to what you really want, rather than what is expected; sticking to what you want and avoiding all the distraction. Keeping aware removes all kinds of problems and if this is the case you will be alive throughout your life rather than just surviving.

MEETING OTHERS

Don't be scared of strange bedfellows; they may not be so different

Hold on to your unique character and this will attract. You will encounter many individuals and can be comfortable with the outcome, because you did nothing that you disliked when meeting them. People meet. They talk. They participate. They have relationships for a while, or they go. This sometimes has no explanation. It seems so shallow, with no obvious guidelines. But why should it have? Only people never realise that life is more enjoyable if it is unpredictable. Doing has problems. To really get the most exciting experiences you have to take risks. But do remember when you are taking them and then you won't be shocked by losing. If there is no knowledge of when things will end, you cannot know if they will run out, so just be comfortable in that. It would be more of a problem if we knew when the end of anything was going to happen.

COMMUNICATION

Taking responsibility for talking

It is so difficult to realise who is the father and who the son, who is the fallen and who the victor, who is the shallow and who the deep, if no one ever speaks. Silence is very important, but it is only a useful tool to allow you to be better prepared to speak. It is also very confusing as to who should make the first move in the communication process. Consider that the son has far more information than the father, but because of compassion, he says nothing. Who benefits? No one of course, so it is also in the interest of the father that the son speaks, even though it may not seem so at the time.

COMFORT

Being relaxed is king

Extremes are very great distractions. Hearing, seeing and touching are useful in developing your relationship to the world around you, but if misunderstood these senses can overbear. Images can lead one astray, because they replace nature with unnatural rules which are open to change; nature is always the same; alive and uncertain. Feelings are real, so which do you know and trust more; your perception, or your feelings? Which is more to your liking, or are they equal? It isn't that Gyerek thinks you should be lazy (in fact to be lazy is far harder than people consider). To be comfortable requires effort. If a good figure makes you comfortable, this involves daily exercise and good diet. If travelling brings comfort, this involves long hours to raise the money. Even being lazy involves some effort explaining one's actions to people who have different lifestyles. The art comes in knowing, which is right for you. The choice is bewildering, but what do you really enjoy? Not what you are told, or expected to enjoy. Benefit from this knowledge at your own speed and in your own time.

FEAR

Nothingness

The dangers which face us are always around us. There is not a place far enough away to leave your problems behind, because you may leave your old problems behind and replace them with a new set somewhere else. It is not the dangers themselves which threaten us; it is the way we face them, hope to solve them, or run away from them. Most of us are so unaware that we continually avoid asking questions, and when we ourselves are asked questions we say we dunno! Why is finding out, or saying what we think or feel, so scary? Gyerek thinks that there is a lot of truth in the old saying, *ignorance is bliss.*

Your problems are as obvious as an on-coming lorry, if you use your eyes and look. Leave the bias of your upbringing and surroundings, and use your senses, and you will see the ups and downs for what they are. Getting involved with situations and people that you are unsure of can make you nervous, especially if it challenges the way you see things.

So don't get involved with other problems. Far more frightening is the way people trap themselves, convicting themselves to a life full of worries and problems. By not asking or answering questions they get nothing. Having nothing leaves them unable to cope with things, as they are inexperienced in facing up to problems and have little information to go on.

There are so many fears that it almost seems as if there is a tailor-made type of fear for everyone who is unaware, or who prefers to have one. Fear comes in all the shapes and colours you want. Once you are aware of fear, you will never forget that feeling, so just accept it and it will not seem so important.

By concentrating on the real concerns - food in your belly, a roof over your head, when you need to rest, a place to sleep, friends that know and like you, your favourite place and the things you really enjoy doing, fear seems a long way away. However, even in the middle of your best times, or even all the time, you can still feel scared; why is this? Because you are lying to yourself; once you have a fear, you have to accept it and carry it reasonably, getting it in perspective. If you ignore it or believe it simply goes away, you have not learnt that the fear is as important to carry as the joy.

There are large numbers of people who prefer to live with their fear, rather than deal with it to enjoy life more. But they would never admit it and some don't recognise it. Do your best to recognise your fears and carry them proudly; use them to appreciate the good things.

GOOD LIFE

Good flows without effort

A good life is based on being honest, true, correct (in all your ways) and on time. It recognises the importance of being gentle and kind and appreciates that all these things can be found in the most unlikely people.

This leads to agreement and consensus in yourself, but never influence the normal rebellious process of discovery in others. People try to convince, decide, ensure, educate and remove the mistakes. Gyerek says let individuals develop themselves as they will.

KNOWING NOTHING

Being open

All things comes from one recurring single embryo. All things, that we know, divide and grow and in the same way all things split and split until all the chemicals and their combinations are formalised.

All things contain positive and negative and balance combines these forces. People think there must be a purpose, but humans know nothing and expect nothing. Saying you would like to know, leaves your mind clear to learn. By saying you know, you don't have the room inside to learn. That's how it is.

VALUES

Ideas are the beginning of the future

Soliders trap and play on their terms. This is known as advancing unseen. It creates the illusion of strength without muscles, attacking without moving, and having concealed defences. War, whether on the battle field, in business, sport, or with the ones we love, cannot take self-respect, but it takes all else. If a battle does take place values, hopes, dreams and humanity are lost. What is right, even with the smaller force, will win. No force is big enough to overcome truth, so why do people try? Gyerek thinks people do not understand that there are no winners if the truth is lost.

Deciding what is important is not an idealist exercise! People are so narrow in their thinking. They believe that concentrating on feeding yourself; aquiring a job, house, money etc, are the practical things individuals should be concerned with to obtain happiness, and that everything else is possible because of that. Gyerek thinks that it is important to be competent at acquiring these essentials, but this is not the essence of happiness. Happiness is derived from self-satisfaction. In which ever form this takes, it may be in acquiring the above practicalities, but it may also include sacrificing income to help the disadvantaged. Whatever satisfies you should be discovered and followed, to truly gain happiness.

SICK OF IGNORANCE

Empty minds are clear to feel

If you are sick of ignorance, you are the sane one even when all others say you are mad. Humans are sick of ignorance and are most qualified to do things for themselves, rather than have people telling them what they should like. Gyerek encourages awareness; the use of observation, thoughts and feelings to obtain the things the individual is happy with; playing, making love, eating, etc, why aren't people sick of ignorance? Why don't people explain the ways of nature, their needs and wants and remove images? Gyerek is sure again that there is no reasonable answer.

TRUST

Trust lasts for ever

Recognise honesty in yourself, family, village, town, city, nation, earth; it is the greatest feeling. You cannot learn it, you cannot promise it; you either know it or you don't.

Therefore observe the family, village, nation and all things for what they are, and see the honesty which is there. Gyerek knows honesty around him, because he looks.

WHOLENESS

Knowledge is quiet and ignorance is noisy

Moving without speaking, and judging information creates awareness. Once you have this awareness it must be moderated to reduce the issues and worries around you. Applying this real understanding must be in keeping with people around you, so do not get frustrated; just be yourself. Hold in your light, your consciousness, and in that way you can live close to nature. Living like this you will have no worry about friend or enemy, whether good or bad or rich or poor. It sounds great and can be so easy, but unless by this time you can believe in yourself, you will not understand how this might be possible.

HARMONY

The secret of being young is to be real.

There is no natural disaster which will surprise you if you are real. You suddenly understand that you are small and weak, but you have the most amazing hold on reality. You may be part of a group or continue to participate in the world of people, but you will have acquired the ability to

remain yourself, rather than be lost in relationships, events, or emotions.

Keeping in touch with yourself allows your nature to instruct you. Be conscious, quiet, comfortable. Any activities which require more output than your energy ability allows will not be sustained, so don't do them. You may interact well, or not, with people, but you will always be welcomed for your honesty by real human beings, even if they do not like or agree with what you do or say. At this point you must realise that being in touch with good and bad, in such a comfortable and effortless way, is not going to produce constant euphoric and uncontrollable happiness. It produces a kind of state of well-being which takes all the ups and downs in its stride so you can be more comfortable, whether you are happy or sad.

EASY LIFE

REPRODUCTION

Humans recreate light, and woman is the vehicle that bears and carries this potential

Reproductive capacity is the start of all individuals' potential and this should never be forgotten. It has always been the case that women and children leave first to escape disaster. This allows the human race to continue, because they will be able to breed.

The reasons for reproduction, however, are far greater than surviving. Breeding is the way all animals evolve, so allowing the women and children to escape gives the best chance for the species to avoid disaster in future. This simple and basic principle is easily understood when it is seen in connection with man-made or natural disasters, but it is less readily seen during our daily lives.

Evolution is widely accepted within the animal kingdom, but the discussion of evolution in connection with the species Homo erectus, (man), is frowned upon. Why is this? By far the largest reason for this bias has been the way people in the past have approached this question. The experiments carried out under Hitler's direction in the Second World War were not evolution. That work tried to pervert nature. This is common in people, but not often seen so obviously.

The sort of evolution which Gyerek discusses is far more common. It is the way each and every one of us has a small hand in recreation, by the partner(s) we choose to breed with. Our behaviour is based on attraction, as in the rest of the universe, but instead of mathematicians trying to explain this attraction, it is psychologists and sociologists. Most of us do not even consider that we are choosing; we are in love, we care, and we like what we see.

So where does this put Darwin? His ideas developed around the unusual. He thought that if an uncommon individual in any population was better suited to their surroundings, then that individual would breed and be more successful in the next generation. Slowly the species would develop through this until either the species as a whole has adapted or there is a new species. Gyerek thinks that this is another reason for the differences between human beings and people. People are not concerned about the substance of a potential partner; they are fundamentally attracted by the partner's looks, or they don't know what the attraction is.

Humans, on the other hand, can sense, or know that a potential partner has substance; a wider grasp about their surroundings and events. They are not continuously talking about their job, clothes, or indeed any matters of image, unless it suits them. They prefer to look behind the veil of image to discover if the prospective partner has the type of human quality which puts them apart; some of the qualities of the masters mentioned earlier. Once discovered, humans will always know one another because they are always honest and will always communicate, even through times of anger and frustration. This is their strength and their attraction.

The individuals who make up a population determine its fate by this evolution. Gyerek thinks that if you want a better world, you should choose to breed with decent humans and not with shallow greedy people. Slowly the political people will become a minority and nature will have a chance.

The final and most important aspect of reproduction was highlighted by Freud, but unfortunately people made it into a science. He observed that the characteristics of the parents' behaviour were often the major contributing factors to good, or (more often in Freud's observations) bad behaviour in their children (the universe recreates itself through the same process). Gyerek therefore offers the two following beliefs for your information:

The way that you were brought up will have a very strong influence, if not absolute effect, on the way your children behave and the way your children will bring up their children.

Reproductive capacity always remains well after all the images of gods and materials have gone.

So choose well.

RECREATION

This is true recycling; everything happens in cycles

Gyerek believes there is no such thing as *creation*. The universe has always existed. Different combinations of personal characteristics in individuals have always been possible. Trees have saplings, because there are trees, they are inseperable. Parents have children, because male and female are attracted, and are of opposite sex. Everything that exists reproduces/recreates, so why should the universe be any different; after all, the stars, the planets and man are part of the same thing; nature. Nature is so special that it makes us, the earth, the universe and all things what they are. Every turn of the cycle tends towards balance after chaos, and chaos for a short time within balance.

This is an infinite process, and each of us for a while has the potential to see this process operating around and in us during our life-time, if we look. Gyerek knows it has always been; history exists because of movement. Movement of man, the earth, the universe and the nature of the universe. This movement will never stop, because movement in individuals, the earth, the universe may die, but others are born. Nature can recreate itself.

This is where you should look for many things, if you wish to change the configuration of things such as matter or energy; people should look at where this happens already, such as in the earth's core, or in reproduction. Methods of travelling through the universe could also benefit from a nature lesson.

Look at the way of plants; if a species wishes to disperse, it recreates itself and sends it out in a strong container, a seed. Space travel could use the same process. Send a number of egg and sperm in a solid container, which could be mechanically fertilized and educated, when they arrive at their destination in space.

Or the second use of recreation in space travel could send an Ark as in the old testament, with all the animals and plants in twos, to reproduce during the journey, to provide the food. Maybe this is how man got to earth in the first place!

Many of the greatest discoveries are waiting, if only we had eyes to see the resilience of recreation. If humanity could, even for a short time, rest from taking and begin to listen to the universe.

HUMAN NATURE

More than wanting something, it is important to know why

The problem with knowing is fourfold. It first makes you despair for the ways of people. There is a great urge to give up completely and, like many others before, just survive, or even give up living totally. But this feeling is totally misguided and mistaken. This book has not just been an exploration of the nature of things and of yourself, it has also highlighted the fundamental differences in the nature of individuals. So do not be surprised by people; if their nature is different from that of humans, it is just how they are. Also, don't be worried that you are any way superior because of your discoveries; it is people who classify themselves by being unaware and greedy. Hopefully by now you should know which you are and what you can do within your life, to minimise the effect of people on you and to increase the opportunity to be yourself.

The second problem is that there seem to be few decent humans around. This is true, but don't be too surprised. The type of life that most people live today does not lend itself to exploring their intrinsic characters, and even after people read this book, most will not even try to find themselves. It is not money which is the root of this lack of attention, it is a seemingly irrational arrogance. This arrogance is like the effect of man-made poisons such as myxomatosis in rabbits. Materialism produces people who have red eyes, who cannot see the difference between; needs and wants, their actions and effects, their choice (mostly lack of) and the resulting lifestyle, their beliefs and the vendors which encourage image, and possibility and reality. People prefer to argue rather than have conversation. There are potentially more humans around than you imagine, but the poison of people (their advertising, their greed) reduces the likelihood of them ever becoming who they might be. You may meet, or may be a decent human, but other humans are difficult to spot because they often camouflage themselves to survive.

The third problem is the emotional urge to go and search for other humans. By doing this, you will be missing the things you wish to do. Understanding nature brings reason to the normal rigour of your life, generating an effortless existance. So let things be. If you have brains in your shoes, and feet in your head (or is it the other way around?) you are more than likely to meet or attract others just like yourself.

The fourth is the way all of us have relationships. The most important fundamental thing about all individuals is that they are weak. Humans will be curious about everything, collect information on everything. There is no way that this tendency can be modified and there will probably be huge problems resulting from action during this learning process. People are not keen to give information. There are two reasons for this; firstly, people do not like to share, secondly, they often don't know the answer. The problems are therefore obvious.

The only real and life-giving force is that this investigation is not stopped, that communication is still open and that you still care at the end, and you can laugh at yourself and the hassles which occur. Why do people wish to kill the hope in others? Who knows what is right? You can accept yourself, others, your surroundings and the events and situations which happen, with all the ups and downs. Humans may have to modify their behaviour when dealing with people they care about. Perhaps the people you care about will tell you to be yourself, then you can. Who knows? But when trying and doing some of these things remember the following. Even if you have discussed your actions and gained agreement, you will only really be able to know how people feel when they react to what you have done or think you have done.

The emotional reaction you receive will usually be totally uncensored, so be careful how you react to it. You may decide someone else's mind for them by reacting badly yourself to their emotions. Your reaction will probably be even more extreme than theirs. So let things settle and continue to participate. There is time to allow this. Be good to one another. This is emotionally difficult, but if you can get through these times and still be there for each other, you will have truly found the reason for existence itself; the ability to live and let live.

Gyerek wishes that this emotional journey is as short as understanding that you need plus and minus for lightning in the skies. The skies are there after lightning; are you there for each other after emotions? Your emotions are like the lightning. They are the same process, but remember lightning is never the same shape and rarely hits the same place, so do not assume that the situation or its outcome will have anything to do with the last occasion you had any similar relationships.

The one assured thing is that if you do see similarity, the present situation is more likely to end with the the same result. So be open to the freshness in events. Things do evolve; understand this and move on. Gyerek recognises that the individuals can have a role; this book is his investment in hope, encouraging individuals to be aware how they could.

So just know who you are, keep in touch with your hopes and emotions, most of all that after emotional attachment with others, you return to your own emotions as quickly as possible and don't waste years, or the rest of your life, worrying about the cost of caring.

Fundamentally most individuals would like a partner as long as possible; some also would like that relationship to help bring up their children. But don't forget that any relationship is unstable because individuals need their freedom to go and discover, enquire, and come home, to be able to go again. Why individuals can't understand and accept this, enabling them to lose the aggressive vocabulary of the feminist and the bachelor, Gyerek just does not know.

If everyone could understand that men and women equally have hormones so much emotional waste would be avoided. A partner can be many things; a friend and companion, a parental replacement, a colleague, but fundamentally a partner is for fun, or breeding.

So when you take on the finery of image, realise what type of partner you are attracting. Who knows what tomorrow will bring, so enjoy today and stay yourself. Tomorrow will then look after itself.

SPEED OF LIFE

Thinking before you move reduces the speed of reaction

Thinking does not bring a life you are emotionally happy with. People try this, but the cost is often so high, that they end up with no life at all.

It was a Monday afternoon when Gyerek met Jim. Jim wished to employ Gyerek to remove some of the burden of tasks which so often slowed Jim down. Jim became so involved with organising Gyerek that Jim could have performed the task himself. Gyerek tried to help, but Jim was only intelligent, narrow in his thinking and often insensitive in his communication. Gyerek left Jim to continue doing the same for the rest of his life. Gyerek was upset at first by Jim's way, but realised that Jim did not know how to relate to individuals and probably was not interested in learning.

Gyerek had thought for five weeks that things would change, but they did not change from the way he had felt after the first hour. He was five weeks behind his feelings. He had waited for something that was not possible and wasted his time. So to truly live as a human you must live life in real time, the time of movement, and this is mostly too fast for thinking.

You must react first with feeling, and then think as soon after as possible. If your thoughts and feelings meet, as they sometimes do, you feel and understand, but the way to maintain this unity is to trust your feelings above all.

LETTING GO

Do not depend on all these ideas

Gyerek could present anything he likes here, but he would encourage you to feel whether these ideas are true and discover them for yourself at your own speed. Remember there are mirages in nature. The ideas are only written as an aid to discover and remember your own thoughts today and tomorrow. Just decide the type of creature you are, and be it.

If this is not completely possible, try it in as manageable a way as you can. Try and express yourself. Use the inate potential you have to help you off the nature trail as soon as you are ready. The consequence of using another's map is that every day you will be saving up problems, which one day will emerge to your cost and bewilderment. So don't depend on others' thoughts, consider you own.

The price of not being yourself is that the very existence of nature is threatened. If you are unable to be your own nature, you will be unable to let your surroundings, the earth, the universe, all things and therefore nature be themselves. If you picked up this book to discover the answer to an easy life, then by now you should be involved with things and individuals you are happy with. Gyerek hopes you do not forget that this process recreates itself every day and you have to find yourself every day and behave as you would every day and do the things you feel every day. Life is very short, and you are a long time dead. So don't waste time unless that is what you truly enjoy doing. But if you don't like wasting time and you don't like what is happening to you and your world, and to nature itself, then do what you do to make it as you want it. Don't give up; stay alive and young. If you die in your thoughts and feelings the numbers of humans will be one less. You will miss how many other real humans still want to live.

RHYTHM

Listen to the music and your timing will be there

There are many influences around us to which we react; our friends, family, lovers, financial, environmental and so on. Understanding rhythm allows us to be in touch with these stimuli, to move with them rather than be at odds. When you are tuned in you gain energy. It seems to push you on to the next thing. You revolve in your character without effort. But when you are off the beat, the flow is lost and you quickly become bored.

The universe is perfectly tuned. So much so, that scientists created mathematics to measure it. But it has not been successful because it is not the correct method of measure. It does not explain why and it quickly becomes boring.

Music comes closer. It has rhythm, but allows deviation, jamming different beats, different combinations of notes and rhythms. Although this also does not explain why the universe is perfectly tuned, but it's more fun. It's easy to move when you have a sense of timing, and this is as much an emotional as an intellectual and physical link. Without rhythm, you don't understand jokes, and nature loves a laugh. Compare the grace of a ballerina on the stage, with the primitive movements she makes during sexual intercourse. Ask the ballerina which is more satisfying!

EASY LIFE

How to live easily

If you have discovered that you can have an easy life, then the only problem left is coping with the enormous enjoyment which life brings.

There are a few important considerations. First and foremost is to maintain your health. You cannot be the person you have discovered if you are constantly abusing your health. So eat within bounds, i.e. sensibly and simply, and don't drink to excess. Exercise every day to maintain the best physical level you can. This will give you energy to do the things you enjoy. Secondly, be conscious of your effort-levels. If you are tired, rest. If you have energy, use it. Thirdly, be concerned by wasting; time, effort or emotions, unless that is what you want to do. Then do it absolutely and get lost in relevant tasks.

Most of all work within your enjoyment and don't be worried by it; once you have experienced this kind of fulfilment it is very difficult to understand how others can accept anything less. This however will be the next nature trail that you and Gyerek will have together. Now you have something to move on to, why not try finishing what you have, so that you can start anew? The only guideline which must be in place is to protect and maximise your flexibility.

This structure must keep intact your fundamental ability to move. It must make distance from clutter, and attract time, space, and the resources to perform your unique skills. If this framework can be established and defended, then you will be you.

MONEY

Making the most

Before the industrial revolution, the majority of the population in Britain, and indeed all other developed and developing nations throughout the world, lived and worked on the land. It was a hard, subsistence type of farming with little or no mechanisation. The land was turned by horse-drawn plough and the planting and harvesting was carried out by hand. With the potential of greater salaries offered by mechanisation during the industrial revolution, the population was tempted to the towns and cities. Today 42 million of the 56 million people in Britain have an urban lifestyle. This fundamental change in the way people earn a living is the reason for many of the problems which we suffer today.

When people were close to the land they understood the limits of nature, they were aware of the seasons, they were honest because their life depended on it. In the towns and cities there were lots of people who no longer had land to obtain their food, clothing, shelter and money. These needs had to be supplied and the distribution and sale of goods and services kept individuals in work. They sold their time to do jobs, which provided the income to feed themselves.

Today, things have not progressed very far from that position. The structure and fabric of modern-day food production in the UK depends on 643,000 farmers and fishermen/women the rest of the working population providing goods and services. Government perpetuates; laws of ownership, market regulation and future initiatives. The individual either works or does not. So how can individuals live within such a system? For people it is easy, because they are commercial creatures, who value little except full pockets and selling their peers the benefits of the products they are touting; all performed in a professional and caring fashion! For humans, however, the story is different. They are disappointed that they should have to experience such a false system, where individuals are as much a commodity as the products they sell.

How does this system allow for the individual potential you have hopefully discovered for yourself? It doesn't. For a totaller, it will probably be more important to know how you market your unique skill in this industrial market-place, which will ultimately allow you to devote time to it, even though it seems as if developing the skill itself is the hard bit.

Without some kind of financial help, such as access to the land (or a gold mine in your garden!), you will never be able to develop your skills. We all need money to survive. So think carefully before embarking on a set path of self-development. If you wish to develop your skill, then get a grant, or a sponsor, or a commercially interested organisation, or relative to help, or you will be unable to use your time to develop your uniqueness.

Finally, if you have no access to resources, just understand nature and accept your circumstances. Take on the disguise required to get by in the commercial world to get your money and live your own way when you have the chance. Just do what you can to have some time for yourself.

SUCCESS

Achieving the unexpected

The measure of attainment can be strange. Never assume that your scale of enjoyment will be the same as the norms for your friends, family, or TV. Choose a criteria of success which is suited to you. If you like the more usual ideas of success such as education, finance, relationships or possessions, fine. But there are others.

You know best the situation which makes you most happy. If you don't, ask yourself what you want; your own scale of success should be related to that. Think. Feel what is right for you and decide. The most useful definition Gyerek has found is borrowed from the description of a village. You don't know where it starts, but you know when you are in it, and this is the same for success.

Men in general must feel as if they have worked for success, yet for women being comfortable during the task is often more important. Nature is successful as long as it keeps its ability to recreate. So stay alive, doing the things you enjoy, for as long as possible. Until people are able to understand that the world's criteria of success is in maintaining its ability to reproduce the diversity and beauty it at present displays the population will never have the ability, to join with nature.

The planet earth is threatened by increasing levels of pollutants (such as; carbon-dioxide, food production by-products such as straw and slurry, other pollutants from manufacturing) and the small-minded meddling of people. The population of the earth needs ever-increasing amounts of food, energy and space. If people could unite with nature, they would realise this imbalance could easily be solved. If resources were used to develop systems of storing carbon-dioxide and other materials in space, in the form of space farms and new industries (i.e. solar power stations), there would be no environmental issues, except those caused by simply too many people.

This is not an impossible undertaking; technology to take items into space can be investigated. Could we physically link orbiting satellites to the earth allow us to move items into space? When ships at sea pass one object to another they fire a rope between the two ships. Items are easily transferred despite the condition of the environment between the ships. Could a pipe-line to a satellite at the correct distance from earth be secured in the same way, to a dome-like structure in space? The same wastes, which concern us could, in space, be made to form covered field. In this way the earth's population could benefit from more of the Sun's energy and we could reduce the number of space-shuttle launches. We shouldn't play with technologies such as nuclear power on earth, when we could work with nature in space, to produce more of the things we need. Again it's only greed and an unwillingness to try which prevents these pollutants/potential resources becoming valuable.

RELATIONSHIPS

Attraction - the force for recreation

The moon orbits the earth at just the right distance to stay independent, but close enough to stay in contact with the earth. They are linked also by processess. The moon affects the tides, and the earth is the nucleus which the moon can revolve around, similar to the way an atom needs a nucleus and a satellite. The space between is also part of the relationship. It is an area between the two bodies. There are forces like gravity attracting the moon and the centrifugal force which is repelling it.

You too can be like the earth and moon in your relationships. Know which forces attract, and those which are pulling you away. You will equally be able to sustain the correct distance as effortlessly as the moon. There is no contract between the earth and the moon; they move because they are linked by circumstance. This is also the case with you, for whatever reason.

The moon seems as if it is totally united with the earth during its journey around the sun, yet clearly it is not physically joined. This is also the case within relationships. The earth is favourably affected by the moon, and the enjoyment in relationships can be equally constant and satisfying. However, the moon makes no promises and neither should you. The future is just a second away, and anything could happen before that, so enjoy this second.

But the relationship between the earth and the moon is not such an emotive subject as the relationships which take place between individuals. Relationships operate in the same way throughout the whole of nature. This is recreation of Yourself. Your partner. Your previous behaviour (in your last relationship), your way of life. Your need for possessions. Your looking at yourself through your children. Your affect on your home. Your affect on the garden. Your affect on the street. Your participation in the community. Your affect on the way you are governed. Your use of resources of the planet and the way this affects all things.

Don't think that discovering the sexuality, behaviour, or methods which your parents used to raise you will help. Don't think that science or religion (in all its forms) will comfort you. Don't even think that reading and understanding this book is the secret. You are the concealed answer. You have the capacity to feel. If this book has been the key which has unlocked the door, it is only you who can open and look on the other side of it. It's up to you!

Forward

Gyerek has hopefully provided a convenient and comfortable trail for you to follow, so that you are able to know yourself, the environment in which you live, and how you could be happiest. He has highlighted a style, by which you can unravel the mysteries of the thoughts and feelings which concern you. If this trail has been enjoyable, follow it again next year and see if you arrive at the same place. If it has not been enjoyable, ask yourself if you are truly being as honest, open-minded and curious as you imagine.

In either case stay moving, be aware, and use totalling as a beginning. Gyerek wishes you blue skies and grey skies, but most of all that you enjoy both.

It's your move.

INDEX

Acceptance	55	Fulfilment	113
Allowing Everything	115	Gentle	107
Anticipation	68	Giving Guidance	111
Applying Ideas	115	Giving/Unselfishness	63
Appreciation	108	Good after Good	72
Being Real	75	Good Life	125
Bottom Line	90	Grass	106
Calmness	58	Harmony	128
Chaos	29	Human Nature	137
Checking	102	Id	79
Comfort	122	Infinite	18
Communication	122	Insight	98
Consensus	100	Knowing Nothing	125
Contentment	85	What to Avoid	87
Convergence	84	Know Yourself	48
Cycles	25	Learning	116
Desire and Discontent	93	Letting Go	142
Differences	93	Living	110
Discipline	60	Lost Control	101
Dispersal	67	Masters	39
Easy Life	144	Matter Is	20
Events and you	34	Meeting Others	121
Everything in us	81	Money	145
Externalities	80	Movement	26
Fear	123	Nature's Way	44
Feelings	76	Non-agitation	31
Finding your way	41	Non-striving	53
Forgetting	73	Obsession	94
Freedom	109	Only nature	82

Peace	105	Space	21
Personal Treasure	59	Speed of Life	141
Polarity	15	Spoilt Easily	101
Politics	95	Stop Searching	88
Popularity	71	Success	147
Recreation	135	Sustainable	54
Reforming	23	Tailor-made	105
Relationships	149	Totalling	80
Repetition	76	Trust	127
Reproduction	133	Unbiased	71
Rhythm	143	Uniting with Nature	43
Remembering	86	Unthreatening	118
Seeing	73	Values	126
Self Respect	70	Wholeness	128
Sick of Ignorance	127	Winning	111
Simplicity	57	Writing is Over	121